D0102392

500 424 004 00

Tommy Goes To 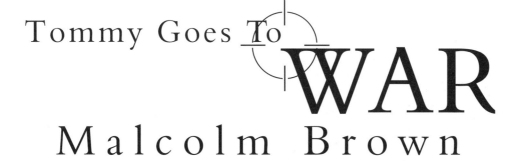WAR

Malcolm Brown

With additional research by Shirley Seaton

In association with the Imperial War Museum

TEMPUS

500424004

First published 1978 by J.M. Dent & Sons Ltd
Re-issued in 1999

PUBLISHED IN THE UNITED KINGDOM BY:

Tempus Publishing Ltd
The Mill, Brimscombe Port
Stroud, Gloucestershire GL5 2QG

PUBLISHED IN THE UNITED STATES OF AMERICA BY:

Tempus Publishing Inc.
2A Cumberland Street
Charleston, SC 29401

Tempus books are available in France, Germany and Belgium
from the following addresses:

Tempus Publishing Group	Tempus Publishing Group	Tempus Publishing Group
21 Avenue de la République	Gustav-Adolf-Straße 3	Place de L'Alma 4/5
37300 Joué-lès-Tours	99084 Erfurt	1200 Brussels
FRANCE	GERMANY	BELGIUM

© Malcolm Brown, 1999

The right of Malcolm Brown to be identified as the Author
of this work has been asserted by him in accordance with the
Copyrights, Designs and Patents Act 1988.

All rights reserved. No part of this book may be reprinted or reproduced or
utilised in any form or by any electronic, mechanical or other means, now
known or hereafter invented, including photocopying and recording, or in any
information storage or retrieval system, without the permission in writing from
the Publishers.

British Library Cataloguing in Publication Data.
A catalogue record for this book is available from the British Library.

ISBN 0 7524 1772 X

Typesetting and origination by Tempus Publishing.
PRINTED AND BOUND IN GREAT BRITAIN.

Contents

Preface

What was it like to serve on the Western Front in the First World War? To cope with rats, lice and endless, cloying mud? To go 'over the top' into battle? To be wounded, or to witness the death of friends? And how in all this did the soldier keep his sanity – and his rich dry humour?

These were some of the questions which *Tommy Goes to War* set out to answer using as prime evidence the words of the men who were there; its attempt to do so has won it a steady and valued readership since its first publication twenty-one years ago. Unfortunately the loss of the film of the original J.M. Dent edition kept it off the shelves for more than a decade, so that its reappearance in this new format under the Tempus imprint is especially gratifying. Recreating the book has also allowed some important changes. In the original format the inclusion of certain thematic sections on various side aspects of the war tended to interrupt the book's narrative stride. By reducing them or weaving the best of the first-hand material they contained into the narrative the text has been given much greater prominence, making it considerably easier to read; something which an author always finds gratifying. Similarly certain well-known photographs which have now virtually become Western Front clichés have been excluded, but the emphasis on unusual, in some cases personal, illustrations and on the inclusion of official forms (something for which the book has been particularly appreciated) has been retained. A major, more obvious improvement is the presence of 16 pages in colour, a reminder perhaps that though later generations often look back on 1914-18 as a black-and-white or sepia war, it was not so to the participants.

Two other changes require notice. First, this new edition is published in association with the Imperial War Museum, a tribute to the fact that – thanks to a process largely begun with the writing of *Tommy Goes to War* – I have now been a freelance historian at that distinguished institution for the past 10 years. Secondly, Shirley Seaton's vital contribution as researcher, without which the book would have been seriously impoverished, indeed would not have been completed in the time allowed, is now gratefully acknowledged on the title page.

One omission in the original edition can now be put right. Curiously, it never occurred to me when writing the book two decades ago that the term 'Tommy' needed explanation. Much could be written on this subject and there are numerous theories as to its origin. Some things, however, can be stated with confidence: that the name 'Thomas Atkins' appeared on certain official forms in the nineteenth century as a stand-in name for the ordinary soldier, that this was popularly abbreviated to 'Tommy', and that the name was given wide currency by Rudyard Kipling in his 'Tommy' poems at the time of the Boer War. The 1914-18 British soldier never really liked the label, but it was ready and waiting and was widely used and understood. In this book it is used as a convenient term of reference, but also and more importantly as a term of admiration and honour.

Most acknowledgements appear at the end of the book but I cannot conclude this Preface without expressing my particular gratitude to Tempus Publications, to its Director Alan Sutton and to its Publisher Jonathan Reeve, for giving new life to a work which will always have a special place in my affections.

Malcolm Brown, July 1999

1 'A call to arms'

As the war which was to last four and a quarter years and claim an average of 1,500 casualties per day began, the Kaiser told his troops: 'You will be home before the leaves have fallen from the trees.' Almost everybody in Britain, except a few hard-headed realists like Lord Kitchener who was prophesying a long struggle that would only be won with the aid of 'the last million men', appeared to anticipate a brisk, spectacular and triumphant campaign. The worry of the would-be volunteer was that the war might be won before he got to it.

Britain went to war at 11 p.m. on 4 August 1914. On the following morning W.T. Colyer, ex-public schoolboy of Merchant Taylors', sat at his office desk in London, bitterly regretting that he had no military connections and thinking angrily of the Germans:

> Would they invade us, I wondered. By George! If they should they'd find us a tougher nut to crack than they expected. My bosom swelled and I clenched my fist. I wished to goodness I was in the Army. I felt restless, excited, eager to do something desperate for the cause of England.
>
> And then the impulse came, sending the blood tingling all over my body: why not join the Army now? A great and glorious suggestion. It might not be too late.

Colyer reported that same day to the HQ of the Artists' Rifles at Duke Street, Euston, where he found 'a roomful of fellows obviously bound on the same mission as myself. I say obviously, for although they were chatting in a blasé way, there was an eager light in their eyes, which betokened the ardent impelling force within.'

He swore his oath and signed on:

> So the great deed was done: the contract with HM the King was signed and I went home throbbing with a new vitality, as (I imagine) a man might who has just plighted his troth to the girl he had loved at first sight.

The same day over 200 miles to the north a young member of the Liverpool Cotton Exchange, Lionel Ferguson, also took the oath. His first war memory was of the clack-clack of door-knockers in Liverpool the previous evening as the police went from house to house, delivering call-up wires to reservists. The next day he went to the Cotton Exchange as usual, found virtually no business being transacted and then made his own impulsive decision:

1   *The men of 1914: new recruits waiting for their pay, St Martin's Churchyard, London. The style of headgear alone is indication enough of the social mix of the men who responded to the nation's call to arms in the summer of 1914. (Q53235)*

> That afternoon I decided to join the Liverpool Scottish. What sights I saw on my way up to Frazer Street; a queue of men over two miles long in the Haymarket; the recruiting office took over a week to pass in all those thousands. At the Liverpool Scottish HQ things seemed hopeless; in fact I was giving up hopes of ever getting in, when I saw Rennison, an officer of the battalion, and he invited me into the mess, getting me in front of hundreds of others. I counted myself in luck to secure the last kilt, which although very old and dirty, I carried away to tog myself in.

Colyer and Ferguson were two of the very first to respond to the joyous, crusading mood which swept Britain the moment that war was declared. A few weeks earlier there had been no sign of a storm cloud on the European horizon; now people seemed to accept the idea of war with Germany as inevitable, even ordained.[1]

There were no doubts as to the justice of the British cause. On 7 August the newspapers reported the speech made by the Prime Minister, Asquith, to an enthusiastic House of Commons, in which he enunciated what was to become the classic justification for going to war:

2 *In 1914 Britain had a small
   Regular Army and a Territorial
   Force primarily intended for
   home defence. The likelihood of
   war required the immediate
   return for all men in the reserve
   to the colours; hence this notice of
   General Mobilization, Army
   Form D463A, dated 4 August,
   the day war was declared.(The
   late Rose Coombs)*

No. B 333   Army Form D. 463A.

ARMY RESERVE.
(REGULAR RESERVE ONLY.)

GENERAL MOBILIZATION.

Notice to join the Army for Permanent Service.

Name *Bull   ag*   Rank *Driver*

Regimental } *15772*   *RE* { Regt. or
Number }   { Corps.

You are hereby required to join the *Training Depot RE*

at *Aldershot*   on *once.*

Should you not present yourself on that day, you will be liable to be proceeded against.

You will bring with you your "Small Book," your Life Certificate, Identity Certificate, and, if a Regular Reservist, Parchment Reserve Certificate.

Instructions for obtaining the sum of 3s. as an advance of pay and a Travelling Warrant where necessary, are contained in your Identity Certificate.

If your Identity Certificate is not in your possession and you are unable to proceed to join, you must report at once to this office, either personally or by letter.

Stamp of Officer i/c Records.

I do not think any nation ever entered into a great conflict — and this is one of the greatest that history will ever know — with a clearer conscience or stronger conviction that it is fighting not for aggression, not for the maintenance of its own selfish ends, but in defence of principles the maintenance of which is vital to the civilization of the world. *Cheers*

We have got a great duty to perform; we have got a great truth to fulfil; and I am confident Parliament and the country will enable us to do it. *Loud cheers*

In this euphoric climate Kitchener's 'Call to Arms', in which he asked for 100,000 men between 19 and 30, was soon fully answered. Before the end of August, he had appealed for 100,000 more and raised the recruiting age to 35. By mid-September half a million men had been enlisted and the recruitment of another half a million was beginning. And the high tide of volunteering fervour continued to flow through the winter and into 1915, so that by the time conscription was introduced in early 1916 some two million men had taken the King's shilling. A.J.P. Taylor has described it as 'the greatest surge of willing patriotism ever recorded'. In Churchill's phrase, this was the rallying of 'the ardent ones'. It is the particular tragedy of this story that so many of these men were to be savaged by the brutal, highly unromantic mode of warfare that was so soon to develop in France and Flanders, and which Churchill, in an even more memorable phrase, was to describe as 'fighting machine-gun bullets with the breasts of gallant men'. But all the horror and tragedy was hidden in the future during the buoyant summer weeks of 1914.

There were, inevitably, other motives mixed with that of patriotism among those who volunteered. For some it was a chance to exchange the dull routine of their lives for the possibility of travel and excitement:

Men of Kitchener's New Army, formally enlisting:

3   *Recruits giving particulars at a recruiting office. (Q30074)*

I had just signed articles of clerkship in my father's office, to become a solicitor, and had to face the prospect of going down to the office every morning and coming back from the office every evening for the next five solid years. And here was a glorious opportunity to break away and look for Adventure — and of course everybody said 'good lad!' and 'how brave you are!'

Lieutenant Philip Howe, 10th Bn West Yorkshire Regt

For young men of profound Christian conviction there was an inevitable crisis to be faced. Could the followers of the Man of Nazareth, the author of the solemn command to 'love your enemies', enlist as soldiers and kill Germans? A young missionary, George Buxton, a Christian of the utmost fervour, who would later become a pilot in the Royal Flying Corps and be shot down and killed near Passchendaele in 1917, argued the case in a letter to his brother in January 1915:

There is no sin in volunteering, God means us to stand up for everything that's right, and if every Christian is going to stand out of the firing line because he thinks it's not for him, then what is left? … It's a great mistake to say Christians shouldn't carry a rifle. I should hate to kill anybody, but then those who are carrying rifles are not murderers, they equally are human and don't love killing others, they do it because it's their duty. Then if it's their duty, it's ours equally in a right cause … We have a 'hope of Eternal Life', then on what grounds can we leave the 'dangerous killing work' to those 'without hope and without God'.

4   Recruits taking the oath. (Q30066)

If we do, won't we rather be held responsible for the blood of those men who are left to go their way without a warning or a Christian example? Especially in this war, where our cause is right, we didn't make the war, the blame doesn't rest on us, Germany forced it and will undoubtedly be punished by God. Such are my views on the great question of the day — 'VOLUNTEERING — SHOULD CHRISTIANS CARRY A RIFLE?'

'The Lord is with our armies,' he wrote towards the end of the same letter, and in another letter sometime later he returned to the same subject: 'We could not go on doing the common task while others sacrifice all for our freedom. We Christians must take up the sword also.'

For most, however, the motives for volunteering were extraordinarily simple: the national mood, the national conditioning over the long decades of Britain's imperial prime, made it inevitable:

We had been brought up to believe that Britain was the best country in the world and we wanted to defend her. The history taught us at school showed that we were better than other people (didn't we always win the last war?) and now all the news was that Germany was the aggressor and we wanted to show the Germans what we could do.

Private George Morgan, 16th Bn West Yorks Regt. 1st Bradford Pals

5 *Recruits putting on their new uniform. (Q 30065)*
 Most volunteers enlisted from strong, basic patriotic motives. As one of them put it: 'I felt we
 were going to do something that had just got to be done. Had not the Kaiser invaded Belgium
 and were not the Germans a bad crowd? Our intention was to defeat them and put them back
 in their proper place.' Private Thomas Bickerton, 3rd Bn Sussex Regt

Morgan's battalion is a specially significant one, in that he was one of many thousands who joined locally raised battalions, of which the 'special inducement', as defined at the time in a newspaper of his home city, the *Bradford Daily Telegraph*, was that its members would 'serve shoulder to shoulder with their friends and colleagues in civil life'. That concept, in fact, dictated their very title; they would be battalions of 'Pals', or, to use a variant adopted by the fishing port of Grimsby, 'Chums'. The industrial towns and cities proved to be particularly favourable ground for the rooting of this comradely idea; hence the Bradford Pals (two battalions), the Manchester Pals (seven), the Liverpool Pals (four), while smaller places such as Salford, Barnsley and Accrington (and surrounding district) also made their proud contribution. Some, such as the Sheffield City Battalion or the Hull Commercials (one of four battalions raised in that town) were 'pals' units in all but name. Once raised, they were accepted into regiments; thus George Morgan's 1st Bradford Pals, as indicated above, became the 16th Battalion of the West Yorkshire Regiment, while the Hull Commercials became the 10th East Yorkshires. But whatever unit the would-be volunteer was seeking to join, his desperate anxiety was that he would not be accepted. Sixteen-year-olds swore they were 19 and heaved sighs of relief when winking recruiting

Temporary.

George by the Grace of God of the United Kingdom of Great Britain and Ireland and of the British Dominions beyond the Seas King Defender of the Faith, Emperor of India &c

To Our Trusty and well beloved *Leslie Arthur Lucas* Greeting.

We reposing especial Trust and Confidence in your Loyalty, Courage and good Conduct do by these Presents Constitute and Appoint you to be an Officer in Our Land Forces from the Seventh day of July 1916 You are therefore carefully and diligently to discharge your Duty as such in the Rank of Second Lieutenant or in such higher Rank as We may from time to time hereafter be pleased to promote or appoint you to, of which a notification will be made in the London Gazette and you are at all times to exercise and well discipline in Arms both the inferior Officers and Men serving under you and use your best endeavours to keep them in good Order and Discipline. And We do hereby Command them to Obey you as their superior Officer and you to observe and follow such Orders and Directions as from time to time you shall receive from Us or any your superior Officer according to the Rules and Discipline of War in pursuance of the Trust hereby reposed in you.

Given at Our Court at Saint James's the First day of August 1916 in the Seventh Year of Our Reign.

By His Majesty's Command.

Leslie Arthur Lucas,
Second Lieutenant
Land Forces.

6   The soldier was bound by his King's shilling and his oath: the officer was bound by his King's Commission. Soldiers commissioned from the ranks were officially discharged from the ranks and then re-enlisted as officers. (Courtesy of the widow of Second Lieutenant L.A. Lucas)

sergeants pretended to believe them. The medical examination was another formidable barrier that had to be crossed. As George Morgan put it:

> I thought it would be the end of the world if I didn't pass. People were being failed for all sorts of reasons: if they hadn't got sufficient teeth, for example: they were glad enough to get them later! When I came to have my chest measured (I was only sixteen and rather small) I took a deep breath and puffed out my chest as far as I could and the doctor said 'You've just scraped through'. It was marvellous being accepted.
>
> When I went back home and told my mother she said I was a fool and she'd give me a good hiding; but I told her, 'I'm a man now, you can't hit a man.'

There has been no time like it in Britain's history. Bands pounding down the streets, patriotic songs endlessly sung in music-halls, a stream of often brilliantly conceived posters, the poetry of poets like Rupert Brooke, the speeches of politicians and other, self-appointed, tribunes of the people, not to mention women with white feathers lurking on street corners — all these and much more produced a heady atmosphere in which amazing acts of personal and communal patriotism became possible. To give one small example: in September 1914 the Northern Foxes Football Team of Leeds met to discuss the election of officers and the arranging of fixtures for the 1914–5 season. One of the members suggested that the whole club should enlist, which after some discussion was put to the vote and passed; the only member allowed to exempt himself was a Quaker. They joined the Leeds Pals, which then became the 15th Battalion of the West Yorkshire Regiment; it would serve in the same brigade and division as George Morgan's 16th Battalion on the Western Front.

Vera Brittain, in *Testament of Youth*, has written movingly of the bitter reaction, later, of thoughtful young men 'who found [themselves] committed to months of cold and fear and discomfort by the quick warmth of a moment's elusive impulse'. And it is inevitably moving to reflect that among those who strutted proudly through the 1914 streets were many destined to lie in the war cemeteries of France or to become the pitiful wrecks selling matches on the street corners of the twenties and thirties. It is moving too to contemplate the flaw, only realized with hindsight, in the concept of the 'Pals' battalions, or of other such units with strong local connections, that those who joined in droves could also die in droves, with devastating consequences for the communities from which they had sprung.

But for the moment the mood was one of high excitement and enthusiasm. The shortage was not of men but of accommodation and *matériel*. W.T. Colyer, who had joined the Artists' Rifles on 5 August, hoping it might not be too late, found himself with no barracks to sleep in but equipped with the most easily recognizable symbol of his new status: a rifle. It was enough to mark him out as a hero of the hour:

> So home I went each evening, with my rifle on my shoulder. As I walked through the streets people looked admiringly at me, and I felt more than ever pleased with myself. Girls smiled at me, men looked at me with respect, the bus-drivers wished me luck and refused to take money for my fare, and everybody made way for me, as being on the King's business.

---

[1] My father, a volunteer of 1915, quoted in this book as Private W.G. Brown RAMC, met a friend in the street within hours of the outbreak of war, who said to him: 'Well, it's come at last!' (The friend, incidentally, was to become one of the war's fatalities.) A great war with Britain and Germany in opposite camps had been, if nowhere else, in the fictional air for years. W. T. Colyer, quoted several times in this chapter, was one of many much affected by an apparently prophetic novel by William Le Queux (*The Invasion of 1910*, published 1906) in which the greatest of all wars was to begin with the invasion of England. When no war came Colyer felt, he writes, 'a distinct sense of disappointment. I felt I had my leg pulled by Mr Le Queux.' Now, four years later, Le Queux was, to some extent at least, vindicated.

7   *Recruits of the Sheffield City Battalion, still in 'civvy' clothes, training at Bramall Lane*
     Football Ground, Sheffield, September 1914.

8   *Platoon photograph, Redmires Camp, Sheffield, early 1915. The men are wearing temporary*
     blue uniforms; only the officer, Lieutenant Willie Clarke, is in regulation khaki.

9   *'Spud-bashing' during training at Cannock Chase, September 1915; seasoned soldiers now,*
     all in khaki. The battalion would suffer over 500 casualties on the first day of the Battle of the
     Somme, with Lieutenant Clarke among the officers killed. (The late J.A. Linsley)

2 'The tents are astir in the valley'

> 'Kitchener's Army!' — a phrase which will stand for a hundred years, and,
> indeed, may stand for all time as a sign and symbol of British determination to
> rise to a great occasion and to supply the need of a great emergency.

So wrote Edgar Wallace, in one of the earliest accounts to be published of the raising of
Britain's Great War army of volunteers. Already famous for his thrillers and with the
added qualification of having been a war correspondent in South Africa, he was a natural
choice for a rousing, propagandist piece of instant history. His book, *Kitchener's Army and
the Territorial Force: The Full Story of a Great Achievement*, published in 1915, gave a vivid if
inevitably uncritical picture of a nation transformed by the call of duty:

> Playgrounds and open spaces, in which the voices of children had
> predominated, now resounded to the sharp, staccato words of command issued
> by drill instructors. The patter of children's feet was gone, and in its place the
> tramp of marching men. Healthy young Britons in their shirt-sleeves wheeled
> and formed, advanced and retired . . . and with head erect and chest expanded,
> went seriously to the business of preparing themselves for national defence
> . . . All over England, in every park, on every common, on every recognized
> camping-ground, were to be seen . . . the white tents of this new force.

The months of training in Britain of the men destined for the Western Front have
usually been described as a time of innocent and happy euphoria. For C.E. Montague, as
he would write in his book *Disenchantment*, this period was 'a second boyhood . . . Except
in the matter of separation from civilian friends, [our] daily life was pretty well that of the
happiest children.' 'Some of us grumble, and go sick to escape parades,' wrote Donald
Hankey, in what was to prove an outstanding wartime best-seller, *A Student in Arms*, 'but
for the most part we are aggressively cheerful and were never fitter in our lives . . . We're
Kitchener's Army, and we don't care if it snows ink!' Even Siegfried Sassoon could write
at this time, in his poem 'Absolution': 'We are the happy legion.'

It would be untrue to suggest that the private letters and diaries of the time conflict in
any major way with this generally accepted view, but many certainly give it a rather more
down-to-earth interpretation. At such a time of national upheaval there was bound to be
muddle, incompetence and thousands of unsolvable problems. High hopes and martial
ardour might carry the volunteer through the doors of the recruiting office, but thereafter
he had to be housed and fed — even a crusading army has to march on its stomach. The

10   *A tented training camp at Frensham Common, Surrey, one of a range of sites developed in September 1914 for the newly formed divisions of Kitchener's Army; Frensham housed the 23rd Division. Camp life was fine and healthy in good summer weather, but conditions soon deteriorated when, as happened in the autumn of 1914, the country suffered a period of almost incessant rain. (Q101685)*

enthusiasm of the most patriotic could easily be strained by poor conditions.

Four days after the outbreak of war, Lionel Ferguson, who had joined the Liverpool Scottish as a private on 5 August, was marched off with his fellow recruits to their first quarters — a local stadium:

> This spot proved to be our prison for nearly a week. We made the best of very bad and dirty accommodation, and our only leave was for $\frac{3}{4}$ of an hour during that evening, then only within half a mile radius, as orders were then expected for a move at the shortest notice. We laid down to rest at 11 p.m. all tired and cross.

> *Sunday 9th August*
> I got out for half an hour before dinner and had a hot bath at the L.&N.W. Hotel, and not before it was needed, as the dirt and dust was awful, also our company had only one tap to wash under, situated about 2ft from the floor in a very dirty urinal . . . How bored I was with life for we had nothing to do but sit on a hard and dirty floor.

It is, however, perhaps fair to add that on that same Sunday Ferguson had been much moved at a service at which such hymns as 'Oh God our help in ages past' and 'Eternal

Father strong to save' had been sung. He wrote, 'The words seemed more impressive this morning than ever before, for we knew not . . . what was going to happen to England and ourselves.' For Ferguson, however, possessing high patriotic ideals did not mean excusing army incompetence, of which there was another example a few days later after his company had drilled for hours in the August sun in a nearby park. 'Hot, dusty and tired, we returned for a late tea to be informed no leave for "A" Coy - just the "Ruddy limit", we thought, but were learning to obey and know that orders is orders.'

The following morning they entrained before dawn for Edinburgh. It was a long tedious journey, for which the only food supplied was bully beef. They tried to get extra food at Preston, but the previous troop train had taken it all. They did get some at Carlisle, and it was here too that boy scouts came along the train to refill their water bottles. In fact it was the attitude of the civilian population that provided the one heartening aspect of the journey. 'The kindness of everybody to troops is wonderful, even the cottage folk all the way up turned out and waved hands and handkerchiefs, which was encouraging to us tired men.'

Next day there was a similar experience for them, this time in the centre of Edinburgh. 'We looked just "It" marching down Princes Street, getting a fine reception from the natives.' But once under canvas, bad conditions again became a constant theme in Ferguson's diary:

Sunday 16th August
The food in camp is very bad, quite unfit to live on; in fact we have to buy porridge etc, from the local women, who sell it at 3d a bowl over the park wall.
Wednesday 19th August
I loathe all this diet and however hungry cannot look forward to the camp food. With all this 'life' one has to eat however and it is no use grousing.

But a few days later he was protesting again:

Thursday 27th August
We had a rotten dinner which everybody refused to eat so we foraged on our own.

Supplying adequate food to such a vast influx of men was inevitably a major problem, particularly in the early days. Clifford Carter, a Private in the Hull Commercials, now officially the 10th Battalion East Yorkshire Regiment, noted the day's menu in his diary on 18 November 1914:

Breakfast	dry bread and cheese
Dinner	dry bread and cheese
Tea	cheese and dry bread

However, by June 1915 Private Peter McGregor, 14th Battalion Argyll and Sutherland Highlanders, could write enthusiastically to his wife:

Dinner today was very good — stew, potatoes, cabbage . . . The officers come round at meal times and ask if we are satisfied — any complaints. Today I finished my dinner and was sitting waiting to get up, when the officer commanding came round and saw me sitting and said: 'Have you had your dinner?' I answered: 'Yes, sir.' He said: 'And all right?' 'Yes. sir.' 'Will you have more?' 'No, thank you, sir.'

But there were other inadequacies more significant than lack of food. Private Henry Bolton, 1st Battalion East Surrey Regiment, who joined immediately on the outbreak of war, wrote in the diary he kept for most of his two-and-a-half years as an infantryman (he was killed on 1 January 1917):

We were generally handicapped by shortage of rifles and equipment, for I was doing my first two months training in the clothes I enlisted in. [He had joined up in best suit and boater!] I received my first suit of khaki (and that a second hand one) the last week in November, my rifle about three weeks after and then another suit the week before Christmas, this time I had a new tunic and old trousers.

W. Carson Catron, like Clifford Carter a Private in the Hull Commercials, wrote of the early days of his battalion: 'Before we got uniforms we learnt to become soldiers in civilian attire with arm-bands. On a route-march one day it commenced to rain and a new recruit put up the umbrella he had brought with him.' Significantly, he added the further detail: 'Our then CO even addressed us as "Gentlemen!"'

It was in fact the high period of the amateur soldier. The most unlikely companions in civilian life found themselves comrades in the tents and hutted camps that sprang up all over the country. Chauffeur-driven limousines waited at camp-gates to pick up well-connected Private soldiers at evenings or weekends. Businessmen rubbed shoulders with bus-drivers, clerks with coal miners, professors with factory workers. This new mix produced one very important change in the traditional make-up of the British army: it introduced into the ranks a large number of questioning men who did not take the arbitrary decisions of military officialdom too kindly and were, in particular, likely to react angrily against what they considered to be a lack of fair play.

Roland Mountfort, a former head-boy of King Henry VIII School, Coventry, who spent four years in the ranks before reluctantly accepting a commission, described in a letter home from Salisbury Plain a minor if genuine case of disaffection in early 1915. His battalion was the 10th Royal Fusiliers, which largely consisted of men recruited from the business houses of the City of London.

Mountfort's company was due for shooting practice at what he describes as 'the rottenest butts I ever saw': reveille was to be 3.30 a.m. the next morning, parade 4.15:

The Sgt-Major was due to wake the Coy, but the night before he had got beastly drunk and when aroused by the sentry promptly went to sleep again. He didn't get up till 4 when he was called by the Cook Sgt who had got the

11   *The members of 'D' Company, 10th Royal Fusiliers, in happy mood while training at Colchester, autumn 1914; Roland Mountfort's Company was 'C', but 'D' Company was also involved in the incident described in this chapter.*

men's breakfast ready. But that gave us only 15 mins to dress, have breakfast, see to our rifles and get on parade. The result was of course that before we were dressed they served our breakfast and before we could touch that they were yelling 'come on parade'. Some stopped to snatch a mouthful of bread and butter, some didn't have time to do that, but anyway at 4.15 the only men out were the 4 officers and the Sgt-Major and the whole Coy was reported as being late on parade.

After 10 hours of firing in 'a heavy and bitterly cold rain', the CO and the Company Commander turned up to visit them at the butts: the latter addressed the men:

He said the Company had disgraced itself; he was once proud to command us, now he wasn't. Leave for the whole company was stopped: fourteen men who went to a portable coffee stall without permission had their names taken and were subsequently given 3 days CB [Confinement to Barracks].

'This rotten Company' was their officer's ultimate insult to them. Stung by the description, with everything soaked through and the water squelching in their boots, they arrived at their tents.

The next morning matters got worse:

12   *Men of the 10th Royal Fusiliers ready for foot inspection after a 20-mile route march. Care of the feet was considered a vital military duty. (Both photographs Mrs Vera Dendy)*

The men on the CB charge insisted on being taken to the CO to protest. The NCOs of the Company consulted together and decided to make the Company Commander apologize for the way he had addressed us or they would resign in a body. All afternoon knots of men stood about in the camp in the way men will when things are fermenting and I'm sure it only wanted one spark of insult from anyone in authority to set the whole situation ablaze.

In the end the matter was resolved by an unspoken decision to take no action and let the matter drop, a reaction which was the equivalent of a climb-down by the battalion command in the face of the quite obvious anger of the men. The Company Commander, when the NCOs went to look for him, was suddenly found to have gone off on leave, and the CO promised to go into the case on the following Monday. 'So everything is standing over; and to stand over in a case of this description is to simmer down and generally settle.' Mountfort then commented somewhat bitterly:

In any other Battn the men would never have put up with the mismanagement and annoyances as we have done. The Gordon Highlanders at Tidworth refused to come out on parade when they had had no breakfast . . .

Similar things have happened in the Gloucesters and other regiments. But we being clerks and not miners or dockers have no idea of union or concerted action.

There were worse incidents than that, in which men died. On a January day in 1915, 12,000 men were marched to a parade ground near Woking to be reviewed by Lord Kitchener and the French Minister of War. Second Lieutenant Ian Melhuish, 7th Battalion Somerset Light Infantry, described what happened in a letter to his mother:

> All Friday morning it snowed and in the afternoon it rained. We left Barracks at 11 a.m. for the Review Ground. Of course the roads were awful, thick slush and mud, and naturally everyone had their boots full of water. Long before we had completed the 7 miles to the ground most of us were wet to the skin.
>
> Well, we got to the ground at 1.30 p.m. Kitchener did not turn up till 4 p.m. and then only went by in a closed car and we did not see him.
>
> Those 24 hours standing in water and slush over our ankles, wet through with a biting wind driving sleet and heavy rain against you all the time, was about the nearest attempt at hell I have so far experienced. The only recreation and amusement was to count the people who fainted and had to be carried out. The engineers won with 32, our company had 8 only.
>
> The scandal was that 12,000 men had been brought out 7 miles from home with one ambulance wagon to hold 6. The remainder had to lie in the slush, some almost covered, until help arrived.
>
> Of course, some suffered from exposure, fortunately only two died.

However, Melhuish could see a good side even to this unhappy episode:

> Fortunately 'it's an ill wind etc.' and it has been shown that the men are splendid. They held the most splendid discipline worthy of the best-trained soldiers, laughing and singing though they were too cold to move their hands. I don't think Germany will win.

It would, however, be historically inaccurate not to state that though there were grievances there was much cheerfulness and gusto as well.

> The men were entirely ignorant of discipline and often uncouth: but they worked splendidly together and seemed to enjoy the novel life. Laughter in the ranks was a very common occurrence. I remember on route marches having to stop my men making excessively rude remarks to people who passed on bicycles.
>
> *Captain R.S. Cockburn, 10th Bn King's Royal Rifle Corps*

> We used to march to and from Lords Cricket Ground and Hampstead Heath singing our marching songs: and thoroughly enjoying the whole business. Our favourite song was 'Mary had a little lamb' and was remarkable for having eleven verses, only one of which was respectable, and that one was usually left out.
>
> *Private W.T. Colyer, 1st Bn Artists' Rifles*

The ultimate purpose of all this was not forgotten, however. For many there was an intense excitement in assimilating the soldier's craft. A newly commissioned young officer in the Welsh Guards, Arthur Gibbs, expressed his enthusiasm in the letters which he wrote home in the late months of 1914, though he was also quite clear that this was shadow-play for a very dangerous reality:

> I am fairly bitten with the military fever and am learning all I can. I spent yesterday morning shooting on the big range. I had never shot before, so I didn't do it very brilliantly: there is quite a lot of kick and the noise is considerable. There were only four firing at once and it was quite loud enough to make one's ears ring. What it must be like in the firing line with thousands going on, besides shrapnel and explosive shell, passes comprehension.

For the present, however, the actual fighting was for most of them weeks or months away. Men peeled potatoes, route-marched, dug trenches, fired rifles (when they had them), stuck bayonets into sacks to the accompaniment of blood-curdling yells, fought mock-battles and generally played at war. Meanwhile countless thousands of cheerful postcards were posted hither and thither about the country, depicting grinning Tommies in every conceivable variety of military activity — or simply as themselves. Pictures appeared on mantelpieces, beside the beds of doting mothers or fond sweethearts, in albums lovingly compiled. The Somme, Arras and Passchendaele were far off.

> These were the happy days when you could capture a village by merely marching into it; when you could hold up a Battalion by merely pointing a dummy machine-gun and refusing to budge; when you usually had lunch with the enemy, each side claiming a victory, over cheese, sandwiches, chocolate, apples and water.
>
> *Captain R.S. Cockburn, 10th Bn King's Royal Rifle Corps*

3 'Tickled to death to go'

Mock battles in England were all very well, but the real battles were taking place in France. Men had not taken the King's shilling to wage war on Salisbury Plain. Suppose it were all over before they had the chance to show the Kaiser what they could do:

> We felt that time was slipping away. At any moment there might be a decisive battle on land or sea, the war would end and we would be too late for the hunt.

So wrote W.T. Colyer, recalling the sense of deep frustration felt by himself and his fellow soldiers of the 1st Battalion of the Artists' Rifles when, in September 1914, they were despatched, not to France, but to garrison the Tower of London. Now their desire to get to the front dominated their thoughts:

> It was the chief topic of conversation: should we get there in time to be any good — should we ever get there at all? We very much resented what seemed to be the popular estimate of us, viz., that we were a sort of mobilized gentlemen's club, quasi-military in character, officially recognized but not likely to be used for any serious military purpose.
> And then suddenly, one afternoon, the magic order came. Battalion to make immediate preparedness to entrain the next morning.
> And our destination? — No official information given on this point.
> Any unofficial information?
> Yes — France!

Colyer's almost boyish enthusiasm was, however, by no means universally shared. For Lance-Sergeant Elmer Cotton, 5th Battalion Northumberland Fusiliers, leaving England for the front was a sad and disturbing experience:

> I was leaving a wife, home and friends and all I held dear to me behind and departing for an unknown destination with all the apprehension of death, wounds and hardships ahead. Packed together 8 per carriage and including full equipment, with blackened railway windows and hard seats, we journeyed south to Folkestone via York, Cambridge, Liverpool St London and Tunbridge Wells.

Before their departure for France, the 9th Battalion of the Royal Sussex Regiment had a final march through their home county, as one of their number, Private Tom Macdonald, later recalled:

> All the villages en route were out to welcome us and say farewell. Many relations of the men were crying. We happened to halt for ten minutes at cross-roads near Bolney and a lot of villagers were collected there and among them was an old Aunt of mine, my Aunt Eliza, who I was very pleased to see. When the time came to march off I threw my arms around her and said 'Good-bye Aunt Eliza'. This was heard by my pals and they all took up the cry: 'Good-bye Aunt Eliza, good old Aunt Eliza.' This was carried back by the rest of the Battalion who took it up. The old lady was laughing and crying. She never forgot that farewell and always in her letters she referred to it later.

Sometimes a departure was turned into a major official occasion:

> I left Devonport on 17 February 1915 by special train to Southampton via Exeter and here we were met with a great reception and were all given tea, also a bag containing a sandwich, orange, apple and cigarettes with the Card of the Mayoress and Committee of Exeter with the words 'Wishing you good luck'.
>
> *Private Henry Bolton, 1st Bn East Surrey Regt*

So at last the long-awaited moment came when the soldier was poised to leave the shores of England for who-knew-what fate in a foreign land. Second Lieutenant Cyril Rawlins, 1st Battalion Welsh Regiment, waiting to go aboard at Southampton, wrote home to his mother:

> Now, dearest muv, keep your heart up, and trust in Providence: I am sure I shall come through all right. It is a great and glorious thing to be going to fight for England in her hour of desperate need and, remember, I am going to fight for you, to keep you safe: the greatest thing you can do for me is to keep cheerful and don't forget to write often and tell me all the scraps of news.

For the future Captain R.S. Cockburn, 10th Battalion King's Royal Rifle Corps, also waiting in Southampton, the eve of his departure was marked by a strangely harrowing experience:

> At the beginning of the war there was an idea, very widely accepted, that men who had been to France, who had fought there and who had then returned to England, were mysteriously altered in appearance. Their eyes were said to indicate that they had been at the front and had 'seen things'.

And there in his Southampton hotel was just such a man, not a British but a Belgian officer:

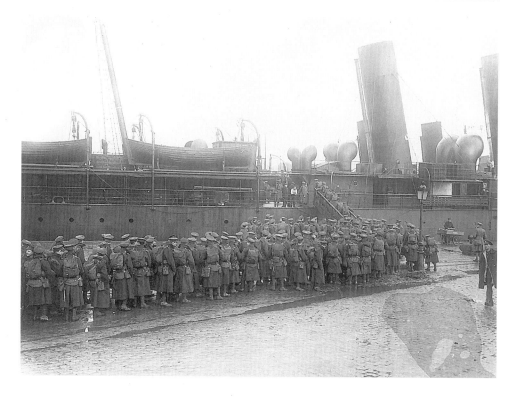

13   *Troops about to take 'the passport to France'; the port of departure is unnamed but would presumably be either Folkestone or Southampton. (Q 33298)*

I almost started with fright when I first looked at him. He had the face of a ghost. His face was as near being yellow as it could be, without being painted. His cheeks hung down like two heavy bags. His eyes were large and grey-green in colour and in them was a kind of haunted, nervous stare, fascinating in its horror. Surely, I thought, this man has been down into hell, and has only escaped by the skin of his teeth! And I fell to wondering whether we should all come to look like that after we had been through a few battles.

Private C.W. Mason, 10th Battalion Lincolnshire Regiment, the Grimsby Chums, also found his enthusiasm somewhat chastened at Southampton:

Whilst waiting on the quayside to embark a huge Hospital ship came in filled with wounded. From the upper deck a voice shouted, 'Are you down-hearted?' to which we replied to a man, 'No-o-o!' Back came the voice, 'Then you bloody soon will be!'

For Private Colyer, relieved of the irrelevant tedium of guarding the Tower of London, embarking for France was exactly the uplifting experience he had hoped it would be, in

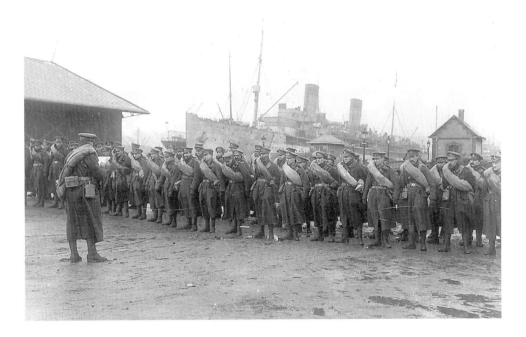

14   *Troops newly disembarked in France; a roll call before the men march off to a rest camp. Again the port is unnamed, but almost certainly it would be Le Havre or Boulogne, the standard points of entry for British or Empire troops bound for the Western Front. (Q33319)*

spite of the fact that the boat had no accommodation for the soldiers and stank abominably of stables and engine oil:

> The romance of it . . . the mystery and uncertainty of it . . . the glowing enthusiasm and lofty idealism of it: of our own free will we were embarked on this glorious enterprise, ready to endure any hardship and make any sacrifice, inspired by a patriotism newly awakened by the challenge to our country's honour.
>
> Nothing could have been more romantic than our passing out into the open sea. As I looked back on the receding coast the sun was sinking slowly behind it, forming an ever-changing colour scheme such as an artist might travel miles to feast upon. The moving boat left a visible track on the calm water, which seemed to stretch right back to the shore as though to remind us that we could never be entirely cut off from the dear land of our birth.
>
> Good-bye, good old England, good-bye!

Second Lieutenant Kenneth Macardle, 17th Battalion Manchester Regiment, crossed to France on a similarly gracious day. 'So England bade me God speed with her sweetest, tenderest smile.' But his first sight of France was less agreeable, and ominous too:

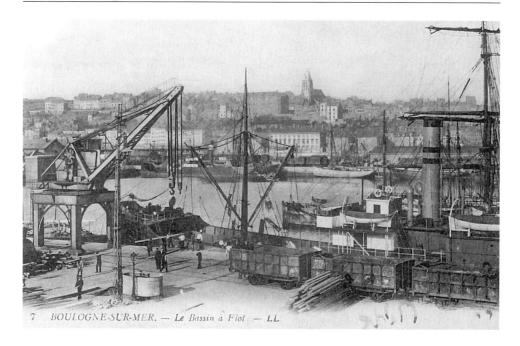

7   BOULOGNE-SUR-MER. — Le Bassin à Flot — LL

15   *Boulogne, as portrayed in a wartime postcard. One soldier wrote of his arrival: 'As we marched through Boulogne, little French boys ran alongside asking for chocolates and cigarettes, and also suggesting that they could fix up an appointment for their sisters for 5 francs!'* Private Thomas Bickerton *(Photograph IWM Dept of Documents)*

Boulogne was hot and dark and sultry. Boulogne was tiresome. While we were waiting at the station a hospital train came in and trench-stained men, badly hurt, some of them looking quite dead, were hurried out of it and away on stretchers.

The war was getting very close.

For most men, however, there was one essential experience of British army life in France to be undergone before they could be pronounced ready for despatch eastwards towards the front line: a period of intensive training at the Base Camp at Étaples. 'Eat-apples', or 'E-taps', as it was variously known to the Tommy, had enough facilities to cope with 100,000 men: here too in the sand dunes near the railway was the notorious 'Bullring' training ground.

The camp was well supplied with Canteens, Cinemas and Concert Parties, but for all that no one ever heard a Tommy say he would like to stay there. The daily march to the 'Bull Ring' and the long tiring hours of training were torture, and men were glad to get away even if it meant trenches again.

Private Clifford Carter, Hull Commercials

16   *The much hated 'Bullring' training ground at the base at Étaples, France, described by one RAMC officer, Captain J.H. Dible, as 'a vast camp with a great concentration of military policemen to the square yard'. (Q33328)*

I think this was about the most detested base camp ever. It was known to all and sundry as the Base Wallah's Paradise, because the people running it seemed to be happily ensconced there for the duration. The various drafts were put through a few days' rigorous training, bayonet fighting, formation drills, etc. Included in the training was passing through a chamber in which Gas had been released (the Instructors used to say, 'just to get you used to the real thing, when you get there'). At the camp one also saw the spectacle of the compounds housing, under military guard, some of our own boys waiting Court-Martial for such offences as deserting, etc.

Private Clifford W. Saunders, 7th Bn Northamptonshire Regt

It should be added for the record that Rouen had its base camp and its 'Bullring' too, but Étaples outstripped it both for size and unpopularity.

It was at the Bullring at Étaples in the spring of 1916 that Lionel Ferguson, formerly a Private of the Liverpool Scottish but now a Lieutenant in the Cheshire Regiment, noted in his diary the following extract from daily orders:

DISCIPLINE, Courts-Martial. No. 1105
No. 15873 Private A★★★ B★★★★★★★. 1Oth (S) Bn Cheshire Regt.
Was tried by F.G.C.M. on the following charge
'Cowardice in the face of the enemy'
The sentence of the court was to suffer death by being shot.
The sentence was duly carried out at 3.38 a.m. on 30 May 1916.[1]

Private Frank Bass, 1st Battalion Cambridgeshire Regiment, spent 10 days at Étaples in September 1916 and kept a detailed diary. It is a cool, frank account, including the good elements as well as those — there were quite a number of them — which depressed and disturbed him. It was, it should be remembered, a gloomy period of the war: the Battle of the Somme was well into its third month, with disappointingly small gains and staggering losses. It was much in Private Bass's mind as he wrote:

Saturday, September 16th
Parade at 9 a.m. and march to Boulogne Station to entrain for Base. We start for Étaples at 11 a.m. On arrival at Base, draw rifle, oil bottle and pull through, gas helmet, etc. Base very depressing. Reports that we may not be here for more than three days before going 'up the line': but could be anything from 3 days to 3 weeks. War of 12 months ago was nothing to what it is now. Only 78 men remain from one Battn. Went to service at Church Army hut tonight — very nice. After service, went round fruit stalls in the Camp. Every day, villagers from Étaples come with stalls into the Camp and hold a sort of mart with chocolates, fruit, postcards and the eternal 'Spearmint'. They seem to think we can't exist without the latter and that it is the staple article of sweet in the English Army.

Sunday, September 17th
Apparently same as any other day. Reveille 5.30. Breakfast 6. Parade 8.00 for 'Bullring' or No. 2 Training Camp. Bayonet fighting with the Royal Scots, 8 of us, including Adams, Coulson and myself, went over final assault and went over all right, I think. After this, rapid loading and firing and then bayonet fighting again. Marched back to best dinner we have had in the Army.

Wednesday, September 20th
Parade 7.45 for Bullring. Lecture on gas. Officer lecturing had been two years here and through two gas attacks. Callousness of lecturers shocks us. Night ops. at night. Didn't know what we were supposed to be doing or whereabouts we were. Strolled aimlessly about. Never been on night ops. which were any good — always a washout. Nobody knows what to do. Officers all swearing and general confusion.

Thursday, September 21st
Uncomfortable night — 15 men in our tent. Plenty of empty tents about but they must cram 15 in one and leave others empty. Another Army absurdity.

Sunday, September 24th
Reveille at 5.30 again and parade to Bullring. Lectures all morning, all our instructors giving us their experiences at the front. All these men seem particularly callous and talk of killing as nothing at all. 'Remember, boys,' one of them said, 'every prisoner means a day's rations gone.'

Then Bass and his colleagues were given the 'bad news' that they were to be transferred from their own battalion to the 9th Norfolks and sent at once to the front. He felt the Government was making a great mistake in moving men between regiments in this way. Thanks to this system, 'lots of men have left their friends and are very discontented'. He commented wryly: 'Good way to encourage "esprit de corps".' The change resulted in scenes of great confusion on their last day, as badges, shoulder titles, even identity discs had to be handed in:

> They allow us to keep nothing. Two men deficient of hat badges and beast of a row about it. CSM of Stores threatens to bring them up on charge of confiscating HM property. Eventually they got fresh ones and had a debit posted to them, in their paybooks, of 2d. Adams lost his pull through and went to get another, quite willing to pay, and QM Sgt. treated him like a criminal — debited him with 1d [one penny].
>
> Drew second gas helmet, goggles and 120 rounds of ammunition. We are absolutely full up now with equipment, etc., and I sincerely hope we get no more.
>
> We go up the line tomorrow.

[1] Since this book first appeared it has become possible, thanks to the researches of Julian Putkowski and Julian Sykes, as published in their book *Shot at Dawn*, to fill in the details which Lieutenant Ferguson scrupulously omitted. The soldier in question was Lance-Corporal J. Holland, and his army number, neatly disguised by Ferguson, was not 15873 but 13857. All other details are precisely correct, including the charge and the time of the carrying out of the sentence. Ferguson's later comment is quoted in *Shot at Dawn*, p.84: 'This punishment was not always carried out, in fact I do not know of another case in the Regiment. One cannot have but regrets about it but such a lot depends on the record of the man and I have known many that deserved shooting'. In fact four soldiers of the Cheshire Regiment were executed during the war.

4 'Up the line'

Thursday, September 26th, 1916
Up at 5.30 to depart for Front at 6.30. Breakfast supposed to be at 5.30. but had a job to get it and when we did, only jam. Paraded at 6.30 and marched to sidings . . .

So Private Bass described in his diary the beginning of his journey to the front, a journey which was to consist of hours in a crowded, slowly moving train, followed by even more agonizing hours of marching. This in fact was the classic progress 'up the line': train to the railhead, after which the Tommy had to fall back on the standard means of troop-transportation in the First World War — his own feet.

Travelling in the troop trains of French railways was, for the British soldier, one of the war's unforgettable ordeals. It was bad enough covering the 50 to 60 miles from the base at Étaples: those who came via Le Havre and Rouen had to put up with the irritations and discomforts of a journey of almost Russian proportions.

Private Jack Sweeney, a Regular of the Lincolnshire Regiment, gave the bald outline of such a journey in a letter home in July 1915:

> I received your parcel on the same afternoon as I left Rouen. It could not have come at a better time as we were in the train from 12 p.m. on Friday night until 9.15 a.m. on Sunday, and all we had in the way of food was six hard biscuits and a pound of bully beef and that was all we got until 10 a.m. on Sunday morning, so you can see how nice that box of chocolates was to me and my chums.

The standard accommodation provided for the Tommy on these troop trains was hardly calculated to impress him with the importance of his contribution to the war.

> We were not expecting to travel first or even second class on the train, but we thought we might have a reasonable chance of 3rd. It turned out we were to go about 7th class; i.e. in plain cattle-trucks with a little straw on the floor of them.
> *Private W.T. Colyer, 1st Bn Artists' Rifles*

Each truck bore the legend:

HOMMES	40
CHEVAUX	8

Which, Colyer continues,

> produces an uncomfortable feeling of a suspense as to whether it meant '40 men or 8 horses' or '40 men and 8 horses'. After 39 other people were duly packed into my truck I was more than ever anxious about the 'chevaux 8' business.

Even without the horses, 40 men in one truck meant no freedom to relax or to stretch tired limbs. Tom Macdonald, 9th Battalion Royal Sussex Regiment, put it pithily in his memoir: 'We were transported in cattle trucks. Jammed in, no room to move. Many, many hours of discomfort and ended up heads and legs everywhere.' That was in 1915, and three years later it was just the same. On New Year's Day 1918 Private Harry Rossall, 73rd Field Ambulance, 24th Division, travelled on a similar train with the added discomfort of bitterly cold weather:

> Arrived at Rouen station. Trucks packed and men lying partly on one another. Someone saw an apology for a brazier by the side of the railway and got it into the truck. Anything burnable was collected and eventually the fire was burning merrily. Then it set fire to the truck floor. The doors were jammed with the gear, packs etc., the smoke was terrific. Eventually someone nearest one door made an exit and shouted to the next van to stop the train. We all had to get out and get in where we could. It was a slow job getting the burning truck shunted away. Nobody bothered and it was left with smoke pouring from it and a nice hole in the floor. They should have had central heating.

If these trains had gone steadily and purposefully on their way they might have been tolerable, but that was something the transport authorities never seemed to achieve. Private Henry Bolton, 1st Battalion East Surrey Regiment, described in his diary a journey of 1915 on the same route from Rouen:

> We started on our journey after 5.30, having left for the station about 2.30, and a very trying one it was for we had a terrible lot of stops. Some of the stops were long enough for us to get out and make tea while other men would be frying a piece of bacon but more than once we had to get back into the train with our water half boiled and our bacon half cooked.

Also in 1915, Second Lieutenant Cyril Rawlins, 1st Battalion Welsh Regiment, did the same journey in what he described to his mother as:

> one of the largest trains I ever saw: 38 coaches of all sizes and shapes: we had two smashes on the way up: couplings pulled out, with a fearful jerk and consequent delays of half an hour, whilst we all got out to stretch our legs and the men made fires and cooked food in their billy cans.

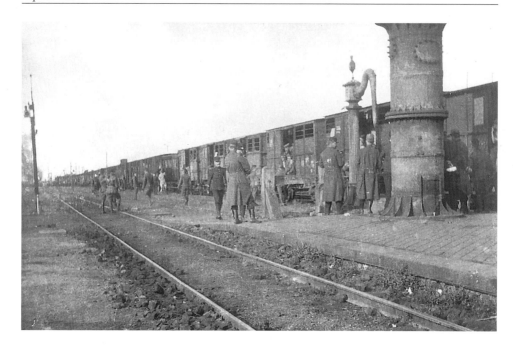

17   *Troop train, largely consisting of cattle trucks. One soldier wrote: 'We were not expecting to travel first or even second class on the train . . . It turned out that we were to go about 7th class.' This photograph was taken at Busigny, south east of Le Cateau, in August 1914. (Q51477)*

These trains seemed to need to stop 'simply to breathe', wrote Captain R.S. Cockburn, 10th Battalion King's Royal Rifle Corps, in his reminiscences. He added that the only relief from the tediousness of one 'lamentably slow journey' which he experienced was the amusing though still rather irritating sight, whenever the train halted, of numbers of small French boys giving vent to everlasting cries of 'Souvenir!' 'Bullee-beef!' 'Beesket'.

But such details apart, Cockburn saw little humour in this ludicrously inadequate mode of transport. Even officers had to put up with desperately uncomfortable conditions. On one winter journey, Cockburn noted, the officers' carriage had not been repaired for a long time and one door was completely broken off, so that the officers had to get out and jog along the line by the side of the train to avoid being frozen in the night. His final verdict on this phase of the transportation of the British Army to war was uncompromisingly severe:

> There was nothing worse for the morale of an officer or man crossing to France for the first time or coming back off leave to take part in some important fight than his railway journey up to the front.

And then there was the inevitable march onwards from the railhead. This is Private Frank Bass's description of the second stage of his progress 'up the line':

We alighted at Corbie and had rations served out to us. Our packs were put on an ASC [Army Service Corps] lorry and we started the march up to Brigade HQ with equipment and rifles. Rottenest march I have ever been on — rotten roads and we had to march about 15 miles. When we got there, found we had to sleep in the open. No one knew we were coming and we might just as well have stayed at the railhead for the night. Army have no consideration for the men at all.

The misery of long marches along the uneven roads of France or Flanders is a constant theme in the letters and diaries of the British soldier. It is one of the curiosities of that war, in which the massed industries of the combatant nations were harnessed to produce guns and munitions on a massive and ever-increasing scale, that the idea of increasing the mobility and sparing the energies of the infantryman by providing regularly available transport for him never lodged itself in the minds of the military hierarchies. Feet had carried the armies of Wellington and Napoleon about Europe; feet could carry the armies of Joffre, Haig, Falkenhayn or Ludendorff. The Tommy was not unaware that there were alternatives to the constant reliance on his own army boots, but he was also aware that such alternatives were rarely seen and even more rarely on hand. Sergeant F.W. Billman, 9th Battalion East Surrey Regiment, confided to his diary in September 1916:

Again we are marching. All this marching is done to save wearing out the tyres of motor-lorries and buses that one sees pictures of, carrying the Tommies about France. At least, so I think.

There are indeed many familiar pictures of Tommies in London buses waving cheerfully at the camera as they proceeded up or down the line. For the vast majority of men, however, it was the long exhausting march, hour after hour, sometimes in rain or snow, sometimes in the equally pitiless sun, that was the norm. They found the going hard and said so:

It was most depressing, plod, plod, legs and boots going on and on and when a halt came we would just fall down, after having a leak, and the pack was getting heavier and heavier. When you took it off you seemed to rise in the air. We had 120 rounds in the pouches and Iron Rations. Full Pack and Rifle. The whole lot certainly weighed one down. In the finish one would be kind of sleeping whilst marching and when a Halt came they would have to kick the chaps to wake them to continue.

Private Tom Macdonald, 9th Bn Royal Sussex Regt

We left Gorre for La Beauvrière. This was one of the worst marches we ever had: it was a blazing hot day, and the men had had no rest for a long time, and we marched nearly three hours without a halt. Several men fell out on the way, and one or two NCOs who also fell out were afterwards reduced to the ranks for this.

Rifleman A. H. Young, 1/18th Bn London Regt, London Irish Rifles

18   *Marching: the basic mode of transport for most Tommies was the Army boot. One soldier
commented: 'The French roads are horrible. Through every village and for a mile or two each
side they are composed of great rough cobble stones.' (Q60734)*

We marched fifteen miles on Wednesday. It doesn't sound much, but when you
think of the heat of the day, the weight of the packs and the state of the French
roads you will understand it was an amazing strain on our endurance. The
French roads are horrible. Through every village and for a mile or two each
side they are composed of great rough cobblestones, about 8 inches square and
not over carefully laid. Apart from the unevenness there is the difficulty that
the nails of our boots step on them as on ice. If two villages are only a few miles
apart the cobble stones carry on and join up the two, so that they stretch for
miles. Our packs I cannot find words to describe. It is a cruel, unnatural weight
that no man should be called upon to carry.

Lance-Corporal Roland Mountfort, 10th Bn Royal Fusiliers

Junior officers often marched with the men: they were spared the weight of rifle and
pack, but for young Second Lieutenant Cyril Rawlins there was the formidable
responsibility of not showing any hint of fatigue or weakness:

Marching: the sun beats down pitilessly. The men have discarded their tunics
and tucked their handkerchiefs under their hat brims behind. No one speaks,

19　*Buses, a much appreciated alternative, though not always present when they were most wanted. The first buses arrived in their civilian colours; soon they were painted khaki and had their lower deck windows boarded up. Ultimately there would be 650 vehicles operating on the western Front, organized in seven bus companies run by 1800 officers and men. (Q6228)*

it is too hot; the sweat is dripping off my eyelashes, my clothes are drenched, my feet burn; ahead the white dusty glaring road: cars race past and we march in a fog of dust. We fix our eyes on a distant church spire: oh how slowly it grows nearer. We can halt there. Passing an estaminet, the heat reflected from its walls seems to strike us in solid waves: the green shutters are closed and thro' the open door a glimpse of men at a table and glasses: a cool interior! A young fellow falters: I take his pack and rifle. 'Stick to it, lad,' as though I was not fagged myself! But I must show no sign: must make a joke now and then to cheer them up. I repeat to myself, 'you must stick it, you must show them how.' I would give anything to fall out: the grassy banks draw like magnets. Oh! to fling myself down there. A little cloud creeps across the sun: we breathe a prayer of thankfulness: the fiery eye is dull for a few blessed moments, then glows again. Thinking of water: the river at home, the aqueduct, the slow black water beneath. There are men at home this very moment lying in punts in quiet backwaters, under the willows.

Standing naked in a tub: my man Bobbet slings buckets of cold water at me.

20   *Ypres, reputedly known as 'Wipers' to the Tommy but more often called as Eepray or Eeps,*
'capital' of the much hated Ypres Salient, with the ruined cathedral in the foreground and the
remains of the Cloth Hall beyond. It was of Ypres that Private Jack Sweeney wrote in a letter
to his fiancée (see page 39): 'It is known to us men as "worse than Hell".'
(E(AUS) 1122)

> Some men have never known thirst, or fatigue: have never known the trial of
> the long march, have never known the blessed relief of rest.

Senior officers could make or break their men on such marches. There are authentic
cases of men dying on the march. In 1916 during the Somme the Post Office Rifles and
the other battalions of 47th Division marched down from the north in paralysing heat,
weak from months of trench war and in full marching order at a rate of 20 miles a day.
There were several deaths from heat stroke and fatigue — to no purpose as weeks elapsed
after reaching the Somme before the division was thrown into the fighting. During this
march a General rode up on his charger to the Post Office Rifles column and told them
some glorious news about a Russian victory — to which a great shout went up: 'F★★★ the
Russians!' The General was so enraged that he ordered the CO to make the men march
to attention for the rest of the day — but his order was soon forgotten.[1]

Tom Macdonald's 9th Battalion Royal Sussex Regiment was fortunate not so much in
its Commanding Officer as in its Second in Command, Major Langdon, who later
became their CO and was, according to Macdonald, 'loved by all':

21   *If Ypres was the 'capital' of the Salient, Albert was the equivalent on the Somme front. Its most notable feature was the basilica of Notre Dame de Brebières at Albert, with its famous statue of the leaning Virgin, secured in almost a high-dive position after being struck by a German shell in 1915. If it fell, so ran the local superstition, the war would end. It fell, brought down by British artillery, in 1918. (Q1399)*

Major Langdon only rode his horse on ceremonials. When on the march he marched with the men, and let any sick soldier ride on his horse. He was at the last of the column and at every halt, which was every one hour's march for 10 minutes, he would go forward to the CO and report if any men had fallen out. Once on our march to the front the CO and he had words. The CO had gone well past the hour for the usual halt. I think he was trying to get to the top of a big hill. Well, Major Langdon, whose nickname among the boys was 'Cushy' (meaning easy), told the CO he had gone past the hour. Cushy said he marched with the men and realized what it meant, whereas the big fat CO rode his horse. This pleased the boys when they heard.

However, even the longest and most tedious of marches had an ending, bringing the Tommy, at last, to the borders of that unique zone around which his imagination had inevitably played through all the long months of training and preparation: the Western Front. It announced its presence from some distance away, as Private Frank Bass, who

22   *Almost at the front, but not quite. This striking photograph of an Australian sentry taken at Fleurbaix, south of Armentières, in June 1916, suggests a close proximity to the trenches, but clearly was taken at a point where such a perfect photographer's target would not also present a target for an enemy sniper. (Q679)*

arrived at the Somme front in September 1916, recorded in his diary:

> We are now within sound of the guns — one big gun keeping us awake all night. Like a thunderstorm all night. Crowds of Indian Lancers about here. As I write this a large observation balloon is floating above us and another has just descended about a hundred yards away. Very large thing, 20' or 30' long.

For Second Lieutenant Cyril Rawlins the approach to the front led him, once again with his column of marching men, through a known danger zone of about 500 yards that was under constant shell-fire. He attempted to describe the scene, sounds included, for his mother:

> Yesterday as we were jingling over the cobbles past the danger zone, sure enough, away to the right came Ponk! Ze-e-e-e-e-e-ee-E-Bang! right over our heads. Again: Ponk! Ze-e-e-e-ee-E-Bang! A little nearer. The road just there is bare of cover, but a little way along on the right was a large barn, shell-holed. I would have given quids and quids just to run to that barn: but I am in front of my column, so I merely glance up in a casual way (what an effort) as if I'd been reared on shrapnel, whereas it's my baptism!

Perhaps the grimmest approach to the front was through the scarred remains of Ypres, that Flanders city crouched behind its infamous Salient which had the most sinister reputation of all among the many towns caught in the coils of the Western Front — its only possible rival being Verdun. Private Jack Sweeney, 1st Battalion Lincolnshire Regiment, had no doubts about its horror:

> It is known to us men as 'Worse than Hell'. It is a terrible place and fighting is always going on there. It was once one of the prettiest town in France [Ypres is actually in Belgium] but now it is only a heap of ruins with dead civilians and soldiers everywhere. Our soldiers dread to hear that they have to go to that place — anywhere except there is the cry.

Sweeney was writing in July 1915. Three months earlier Lance-Sergeant Elmer Cotton, 5th Battalion Northumberland Fusiliers, had arrived at the front through this same 'terrible place' and found it a sobering introduction to the harshness of war:

> By the time we arrived at the outskirts of Ypres the traffic of ammunition and ambulance wagons had ceased and we were alone on the road. The only noise we heard was the echo of our own steps and the occasional roar of a gun or a bursting shell. Suddenly we came across a corpse lying across the pavement and the gutter — it was the body of a peasant - his bundle was lying some yards away having been precipitated forward when he fell. Just over the canal bridge a timber wagon and two shattered horses came into view and we walked through the blood of these noble animals as we passed them on the road. We were now in the town proper — everywhere nothing but ruins could be seen — not a house but was either shattered by shells or gutted with fire. Many walls leaned at dangerous angles into the streets and in the dim light of night each ruin seemed to me to represent the work of some grinning demon who was lurking in hiding behind these ghostly houses. On our way we passed more dead horses, which in many cases were in a state of decomposition and emitted a fearful odour of rottenness.

It was in this setting that Cotton's battalion had its first taste of war — a random German shell:

> My back and pack were struck by a shower of debris and flying dirt while quite a number of men fell and bled for their country. Jack Duncan was in front of me and he received a severe wound from this, our first shell. He was carried onto the pavement and left for the attention of the doctor.

Tommy had arrived at his war.

---

[1] I am indebted to the late Wing Cmdr Shewry, Post Office Rifles Association, for this story.

5 'In the trenches'

My dear Mother,

I am writing this in the trenches. I came up last night after travelling and messing about Belgium for 12 hours. I am surprised to find how quiet it is here. Except for sniping there is nothing doing.

We are in good trenches and hold a good position. It was a fine sight coming up last night to see all along the line as far as you could star shells going up. It was like a firework display.

I was surprised to find that far from being in a funk as I expected I did not mind coming up at all. It is not at all bad here because there are plenty of funk holes if the Bosche gets really nasty.

So wrote Second Lieutenant Geoffrey Lillywhite, 9th Battalion East Surrey Regiment, describing his introduction to the front line in May 1916. Private Jack Sweeney achieved that distinction as early as November 1914:

Well, dad, I have been in the trenches from last Friday until Tuesday and would have enjoyed it very much only for the Rain which made us look like Mudlarks. We had a few narrow escapes — last Sunday the Germans sent us a few presents from the Kaiser, they were Shrapnel Shells or as we call them Jack Johnsons, [heavy shells that gave off black smoke, nicknamed after a famous Negro pugilist] they came very near our trenches but never hurt anybody, and the boys were laughing every time one Bursted, there seems to be no Fear in the old Lincolns. No one seems to Realize it is active Service.
P.S. We get a nice Drop of Rum every day.

'The trenches': there can be little doubt that this phrase was the most emotive to emerge from the vocabulary of the First World War. For the generation of 1914–18 — as indeed for every generation since — the words had and have a unique ring. To have been 'in the trenches' put a permanent mark on a man: he had been admitted to a special, private world, the reality of which, as many were aware at the time, could only be fully understood by those who had been part of it. Men outside that fellowship longed and feared to join it; those inside it tended to 'buck' to their less favoured comrades about their experiences within it. Private W.T. Colyer expressed the typical reaction of the newly arrived soldier awaiting his blooding: 'Since being here have listened to at least 158 ghastly stories of the firing line from chaps who have just come from it. Want to go home!'

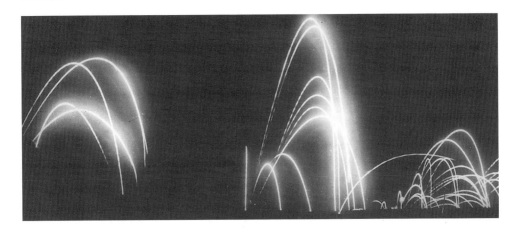

23   *The Western Front at night; star shells illuminating No Man's Land — precisely the kind of
      scene described opposite by Lieutenant Lillywhite. The front could have an uncanny beauty at
      such times, but the purpose was strictly military; both sides wanted to know what the other was
      up to under cover of darkness. Photograph taken near Beaumont-Hamel, Somme, 2 July
      1916. (Q757)*

But there was no mistaking the fascination of that now-so-near Western Front. Colyer
wrote of his billet near St Omer, into which he and his fellow Artists' Rifles were moved
on their way 'up the line', 'It had been occupied by French poilus [French infantrymen]
who had left two days before for the trenches; and such was the magic glory of that word
"trenches" that we were proud to occupy their beds.'

The phrase 'the trenches', in fact, covered a unique reality. The war of brisk and
spectacular movement, as envisaged at the outset in August 1914, lasted only a matter of
weeks. By the winter of 1914–15 a continuous line of trenches ran some 450 miles across
Europe from the Belgian coast to the frontier of Switzerland. There had been trench
fighting in other wars, notably the American Civil War, but nothing on this scale. As
Churchill wrote in his book *World Crisis*:

> All the wars of the world could show nothing to compare with the continuous
> front which had now been established . . . It was certain that frontal attacks
> unaccompanied by turning movements on the flank would be extremely costly
> and would probably fail. But now, in France and Flanders for the first time in
> recorded experience there were no flanks to turn . . . Neutral territory or salt
> water barred all further extension of the Front, and the great armies lay glaring
> at each other at close quarters without any true idea of what to do next.

For much of four years the trenches were to remain more or less along the line established
in those first traumatic months. Salients would be pinched out here and there; the 'Big
Pushes' of 1916 and 1917 would throw the Germans back over a few miles of snarled up
countryside; the Germans would retaliate in kind in a series of great stabs in the spring of

24   *Routine trench scene: Lancashire Fusiliers in the front line opposite Messines, January 1917. The sentry is looking through a box periscope. The presence of the photographer and the casual attitude of the soldier on the left serve as a reminder that Western Front life was as much about boredom as about bravery. (Q4654)*

1918; occasionally the German commanders would alter the geography of the front by retiring to better positions (notably on the Somme in early 1917) - but for the most part the line drawn with astonishing swiftness in the autumn of 1914 held until the final breakthrough in the summer of 1918. When Sergeant F.W. Billman, 9th Battalion East Surrey Regiment, noted in his diary in the Loos salient on 25 October 1916, 'Here exactly thirteen months after, we are holding trenches on the same ground that we fought on, on the memorable 25th and 26th September 1915', he was chronicling a by no means extraordinary experience. The front had its perpetual shifts and spasms, but the same names — the same towns, villages, hills, woods, rivers, streams — occurred again and again in the story. The war in the west in fact resolved itself into a static, apparently interminable slogging-match, the essential element of which was (to quote Churchill once again) 'ramparts [hundreds of] miles long, ceaselessly guarded by millions of men, sustained by thousands of cannon'.

'The trenches', therefore, became the classic experience of this war and the classic location. Many of the most famous paintings, poems, novels and plays which it produced were set, inevitably, in or around the trenches. Whenever people in Britain — or people of the other major western combatants for that matter: France, Germany, the United States — think of the world conflict of 1914-18, they think first and foremost of the trenches of the Western Front.

25   *'Funk-holes' in the trenches: the men sheltering in them are soldiers of the Border Regiment in Thiepval Wood, on the Somme, in 1916. (Q872)*

The system favoured by the British consisted of three lines of trenches: front line, support and reserve. Barbed wire entanglements lay between the front-line trenches and No Man's Land; while on the other side of No Man's Land, which might be anything from 25 yards to half a mile (the average was 250 yards), was the enemy, behind his own wire and bedded down in his own particular trench system. Communication trenches, roughly at right angles to the three basic lines, linked them together and led back to the safer areas behind. Trenches were built in zig-zags to reduce the effect of shellfire. Here and there little trench extensions ran out, for snipers, for example, or more humbly, and on the 'home' side, for latrines. Dugouts were normally (though by no means exclusively) for officers or senior NCOs: ordinary soldiers often had to make do as best they could in funk-holes (holes carved out of the side of the trench) or under waterproof sheets. The Germans built splendid dugouts for their soldiers, but then they intended to stay where they were, whereas the British intention was to shift them out and send them packing. Comfortable quarters, which might encourage the Tommy to settle down and 'live and let live', were therefore not encouraged.

An infantry battalion permutated through three basic locations: in the line (that is, in the front and support trenches), in billets (usually some ruined village or farm just behind the line) where they would act as local reserves, or in a rest camp clear of the fighting zone. A typical pattern would be a fortnight spent commuting between the line and the billets,

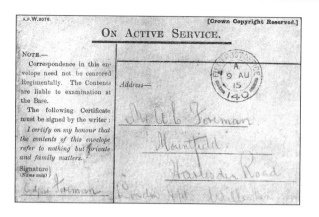

[Crown Copyright Reserved.]

26, 27 *Arrival in the vicinity of the trenches clearly called for*
speedy reassurance to loved ones back home. The Field
Postcard, which could be filled in and signed in seconds
and was not submitted to censorship, provided a limited
but effective means of achieving this end. As one Tommy stated in a letter home: 'Dear Dad
and Mother, I'm afraid you must be getting a bit worried because I haven't written you for
some time, but really I find it very difficult to get a letter off while in the trenches and it's so
easy to send a field p.c.' (Imperial War Museum Dept of Documents)

followed by six days out at rest. Relief of battalions in the line was always carried out at
night; in fact, most activities at the front were, for obvious reasons, nocturnal. The artillery
was ranged behind the trenches: their task, very broadly, was to pound the enemy lines
with shrapnel and high explosive and, ultimately, to prepare the way for the advance of the
infantry. They worked in close collaboration with the infantry: their Forward Observation
Officers and signallers (the latter endlessly paying out their bales of telephone wire) were
always to be seen in the front-line trenches.

Life in the line was not one of constant furious activity: far more often than not it
consisted of the dreary round of trench routine. There were 'cushy' trenches and quiet
times as well as appalling conditions and moments of terrible violence: 'hell let loose' was
a favourite Tommy description for such times. On average a British battalion (at its
maximum a thousand strong) lost about 30 men a month through death, wounds and
sickness. In big set-piece battles, of course, battalions could and occasionally did, suffer
virtual annihilation.

The Grimsby Chums, more formally the 10th Battalion Lincolnshire Regiment, had
their first taste of trench life near Armentières in February 1916. Major Walter Vignoles
wrote an upbeat account of it in a letter home:

> It has been quite an interesting experience and our men were very bucked and
> quite enjoyed it, and I must say I did too. The trenches were on the whole in very
> good condition and there are wooden footboards practically everywhere, and
> with the dry weather too, it was really quite comfortable. One could not QUITE

get a bath! as of course everything has to be carried up to the trenches by hand, but apart from that one could carry on, at least the officers could, very nearly as well as in camp, with the one exception that one has to sleep in one's clothes. We had a very quiet time, and I will say that the Boche behaved in a very gentlemanly-like manner while we were in, and did not give any shells nor any of his fancy contrivances only rifle and machine gun fire. One has to look after the top of one's head, as they are very expert at making the bullets skim the top of the parapet, but THEY DID NOT HIT ANYONE IN MY COMPANY.

The snipers are always busy, but they do not hit what they aim at by a long way. It is queer to hear the bullets snapping overhead, but usually there is no danger, as one is behind thick parapets or in dugouts. They say 'every bullet has its billet' — that is true, but it is nearly always in Mother Earth.

In the daytime there is not much firing, but as it begins to get dusk, the men start to fire over the parapet, a few shots at a time; this is usually kept up during the night, sometimes it dies away, and then we suspect the Boche is working in front of his parapets, or up to some mischief!

While the rifle fire keeps spluttering away quietly, a machine gun suddenly opens — 'rat-tat-tat' and the bullets come snapping overhead or 'tap-tap-tap' against the parapet, and we try hard to see from whence the gun is firing. We see the flashes and take a compass bearing so as to be able to look at the place next day, and if it is located ask the guns to knock it out.

In a letter written after a further spell in the line; Major Vignoles described the basic pattern of trench routine:

At dawn we 'stand to arms', every one turning out. When it is light, all rifles are cleaned and inspected, and the men have a tot of rum. Then breakfast, after which I let them turn in to sleep till dinner, with the exception of the day sentries, just a few men watching the enemy's line through periscopes. After dinner the men turn out for work in repairing periscopes, etc., and put in about three hours at that. We 'stand to' again at dusk. After dark, we have to get over the parapet to do any repairs that may be required to the wire entanglements, or repairs to the front of the parapet. In the salient here there is a good deal of work to be done, and there are several places where the trenches are old and broken, from whence one can peep at the enemy; we filled and put in position nearly 4000 sandbags while we were in the trenches.

Conditions had not been quite so 'cushy' as on their previous visit thanks to a fall of snow on the first of their four nights in the line. Vignoles felt particularly sorry for the 'poor fellows on sentry go':

We have a certain number of sentry groups on duty in the front line trench; each group consists of six men, two keeping watch while the others sit on the firestep, trying to sleep or walking about trying to keep warm. The two on the

Infantry marching order. Going into battle infantrymen normally carried over 60 pounds of equipment, including such items as picks, shovels, wire cutters and, of course, bombs.

Extract and comment from the 1915 Notebook of Elmer Wilfred Cotton, Private, Lance Sergeant and Sergeant of the 5th Battalion Northumberland Fusiliers:

What an infantry soldier carries:
On his body:

1 pair of boots
1 pair of braces
1 service cap
1 pair drawers
1 pair service trousers
1 pair puttees
1 service jacket
1 field dressing
1 service pay book
1 identity disk
1 clasp knife
1 shirt
1 vest (in winter only)
1 pair socks
pouches, basic equipment and belt
2 smoke helmets
1 iodine in bottle
1 waterproof sheet
1 cardigan jacket or waistcoat (in winter)
1 mess tin and cover
1 rifle and sling
1 oil bottle
1 pull through
1 bayonet and scabbard
1 entrenching tool head
1 entrenching tool helme
1 entrenching tool carrier
1 water bottle filled with water
1 haversack
1 valise and supporting straps
150 rounds — 303 cartidges

28, 29   Infantry Marching Order: What Tommy Took to the Trenches
   Note: the equipment shown above includes a steel helmet, which is not in Cotton's list. These were not introduced until early 1916. (Q7508, Q30217)

In Valise:

1 cap comforter
1 holdall containing
    1 hussif
    1 toothbrush
    1 razor
    1 comb
    1 shaving soap
    1 pair spare braces
    1 piece soap
2 pairs socks
1 shirt
1 towel
1 pair drawers
1 vest (in winter only)
1 greatcoat
1 blanket (in winter)

In Haversack:

1 table knife
1 table fork
1 dessert spoon
1 tin bully beef   } Emergency rations
1 tea and sugar   } known as Iron Rations
1 lot of biscuits   }

'The amount of kit and equipment carried by an infantryman makes up an almost impossible weight. It proves a terrible burden on the march, the shoulders and back ache severely; a route march being thus made into a most torturous operation . . .'

lookout change every hour so that each man has one hour on and two off. It is not so bad in warm weather, but rotten in winter or in snowy weather, as they are not allowed to go into their dug-outs during their time off, the reason being that they are so tired that once asleep in a dug-out it would probably be impossible for the other men to wake them in case of an attack. The Boche might get into the trench in a surprise rush and they would very likely be killed in their sleep in their dugouts. That is what has happened to the Boche in some of OUR raids.

For some men trench life soon became a routine like any other. Having spent almost 10 months in France Sergeant F.W. Billion of the East Surrey Regiment noted in his diary in June 1916: 'After six days out at rest we came back into Brigade reserve for six more and then up into the line again. It gets just like going to an ordinary day's work.' But the Western Front was in fact a very extraordinary place, with the perpetual hazard even in the quiet times of death or maiming from a sniper's bullet or a sudden stray shell. Billman himself was well aware of such dangers because of an incident of which he had been an exceptionally fortunate witness earlier that year on Good Friday:

> I had a very narrow escape from death, by a shrapnel shell bursting over me, while talking to three other chaps in the trench. One of these was killed outright, and the other two were very badly wounded, and I was left standing there, untouched. It was the only shell that came over that part of the line that day and as long as I live to see 'Good Fridays' I shall remember that. Such a thing as that is not reported in the papers each day, while the official news says, 'All quiet on the Western Front'.

Lance-Sergeant Elmer Cotton, 5th Battalion Northumberland Fusiliers, recorded a similar event at Zillebeke, near Ypres, in May 1915:

> Imagine a bright May morning and a platoon (about 55 men) busily engaged in washing, cleaning up, cooking and some sleeping. Suddenly a tremendous explosion, a deathly stillness as if all were paralysed, then fearful screams and groans and death gasps. What had happened? A high explosive German shell had fallen right into a wide part of the trench where many men had been. The sight of the wounded shedding their blood from gaping wounds and their agonized cries — one asking to be shot — would have convinced any humane man that war is an impossible way of settling national questions — or it will be in the near future. It was on May 2nd that this incident took place and this single high explosive shell killed 7 and wounded 18 — yet the day before 400 shells came over and dropped immediately behind this trench within 10 yards and no one was hurt — but this one shell bursting right in the trench accounted for a total of 25 men. The trench after the dead and wounded were removed presented a ghastly sight — it was red with blood like a room papered in crimson while equipment lay everywhere.

6 'Rats as big as rabbits'

Private Kenneth Garry, of the Honourable Artillery Company (a regiment of the Territorial Force consisting of two artillery batteries and one infantry battalion) wrote a jaunty account of his first experience of the trenches to his 'Dearest Mother' in January 1916. As an infantryman he went into the line fully loaded:

> We had two days' rations to take, and the 150 rounds of ammunition we always carry. I only took an extra pair of socks, but I wished before I got back that I had taken three extra pairs. We wore our great coats, with full equipment on top of this. Our mack we put on top of the pack. Our water bottle was full and of course we carried our mess tin, also mug and cutlery. The one blanket we were allowed to take was rolled in the ground sheet, and slung like a horse collar round our necks. I carried in addition my pocket primus, and a tin of paraffin, two small tins of Heinz baked beans, vaseline (three tubes, one each of pure white, capsicum and carbolated), a Tommy's cooker and a tin of re-fill; a pair of gloves mittens and a muffler (in my greatcoat pocket). Beside this, we carried our rifle. I wish you could have seen us. We looked like animated old clothes shops.

As behind the line, so in the line the inevitable basic means of transportation was Tommy's feet. Mule-drawn limbers or pack-mules would bring the necessities of trench life to a dump some distance behind the front, but from that point forward everything — equipment, guns, ammunition, sandbags, screw-pickets, barbed wire, duck-boards, food, water - had to be carried by manpower and almost invariably in the dark.

Major Vignoles of the Grimsby Chums expressed in a letter home his sympathy for the hard lot of the ordinary soldier:

> The men are very fit on the whole but they have a rough time going in and leaving the trenches, carrying heavy loads, slipping and scrambling about, and, I am sorry to say, cursing as a rule in a language that would make a bargee turn pale with envy, but it doesn't mean anything! No 'arm!

Feeding the troops in the trenches was never an easy problem, though like all other aspects of service life it had its regular routines, as Private Harold Horne, 6th Battalion Northumberland Fusiliers, recalled:

30 *Stew for dinner: men of the Lancashire Fusiliers being served standard front-line fare, opposite Messines, 1917. Trench food was the butt of much humour and criticism but there were times when it could seem the food of the gods. One officer wrote: 'Did not a mess-tin of stew or a tot of rum, or whisky and water in a tin mug taste more like divine nectar than the best champagne drunk out of the finest cut glass?' (Q4843)*

Ration parties from each company in the line went to carry back the rations which were tied in sandbags and consisted, usually, of bread, hard biscuits, tinned meat ('bully') in 12oz. tins, tinned jam (Tommy Ticklers plum and apple), tinned butter, sugar and tea, pork and beans (baked beans with a piece of pork fat on top), cigarettes and tobacco.

Sometimes we got 'Maconochie Rations'. This was a sort of Irish stew in tins which could be quickly heated over a charcoal brazier. This was quite good at first but one got satiated before long.

When it was possible to have a cookhouse within easy reach of trenches fresh meat, bacon, vegetables, flour, etc, would be sent up and the cooks could produce reasonably good meals and food and tea was sent along the trenches in 'dixies' (large iron containers the lid of which could be used as a frying pan). In 1916 large containers on the thermos principle, which could be carried on the back, appeared in which the hot tea or stew could be carried up to the trenches from

31   *One of the highlights of Western Front life: the arrival of post and parcels from home. Private Peter McGregor wrote to his wife: 'I have been very lucky in the way of letters and parcels — folks seem to be taking a new interest in me since I left for the front.' (Q1152)*

Battalion rear HQ where the cooks could work under better conditions.

In winter there was a ration of rum, one or two tablespoons per man; this was a strong, black spirit which was usually issued during the morning 'stand-to': it was very welcome on a cold winter's morning. It was supplied in a 'grey hen', a heavy earthenware jar marked SRD (translated as Service Rum Department).

In summer there was a ration of neat lime juice supplied in the same kind of jar. There were reports that some unfortunate unit had received this in winter in mistake for rum nearly causing a mutiny.

Water was sent up the line in petrol cans. We were not supposed to use untreated water so each battalion had water carts and the medical officer was responsible for ensuring that it was chlorinated before use.

Food in the trenches had an eternal sameness about it. As Private W. Carson Catron, of the Hull Commercials, put it, his principal memory of trench food was of 'the monotony of bully beef and biscuits, and plum and apple jam and biscuits, washed down with tea flavoured from the previous meal, cooked in the same container as the water was boiled, onion being predominant'.

32   *Christmas dinner in a shell hole at Beaumont-Hamel, Somme, 25 December 1916. Thanks to parcels from home such meals could often be served to an almost standard seasonal menu. (Q1630)*

The soldier was not likely to starve, for if the worst came to the worst he could always fall back on his iron rations. These, however, were only to be eaten in extremis; when Tom Macdonald, 9th Battalion Royal Sussex Regiment, asked his officer 'when do we eat our iron rations?' he received the following memorable reply: 'You don't eat your Iron Rations until your belly button hits your back bone and your hip bones show out of your trousers!'

In the circumstances, there was inevitably much reliance on parcels sent from home. One of the positive aspects of service on the Western Front, as opposed to such other foreign fields as Salonika, Italy or the Middle East, was that mail, post and parcels came very quickly to the soldier in the trenches. It was possible to ask and receive within days.

> If you can manage it occasionally cakes and sweets (cheap ones of the hard nature) would be quite welcome for the little dugout mess. They would have to be packed securely though because they come by a rough road.
>
> *Second Lieutenant Geoffrey Lillywhite, 9th Bn East Surrey Regt*

> I have got a cardboard box with extra food, which I am husbanding very carefully. I have got some Bivouac cocoa and beef tea squares, which are excellent and really invaluable. Will you send out a lot more of both as soon as possible? Even if I don't want them, the men would be delighted to have them, as they haven't got any extra delicacies.
>
> *Second Lieutenant Arthur Gibbs, 1st Bn Welsh Guards*

Lieutenant Gibbs's last statement was perhaps a shade sweeping; parcels were by no means exclusive to officers:

> On June 20th we were working all night taking ammunition to the guns and the next day, being my 21st birthday, I slept all day, as we were to go out again the following night. Somebody woke me up about midday and handed me a parcel from home; I opened it and found it contained cakes, which I shared out amongst the others, who wished me many happy returns of the day, then I went to sleep again.
>
> *Driver R.L. Venables, Royal Field Artillery*

> This is a red-letter day. My parcel came this morning with a tin of peaches, loaf and butter, fish paste, tobacco, sleeping helmet, chocolate, a pair of socks and a towel. Had peaches for sweet at dinner and fish paste for tea. Grand.
>
> *Private Frank Bass, 9th Bn, Norfolk Regt*

> If you are sending any eatables amongst yourselves, you might put in some tooth powder as I have not cleaned my teeth for 3 weeks, also should like some of your jam if you have any as it makes the hard biscuits eat better, especially on Sundays.
>
> *Private A.H. Hubbard, London Scottish*

It is, of course, undeniable that officers fared better, particularly those with the right social connections. Second Lieutenant Cyril Rawlins listed in a letter home some of the delicacies which had enriched his life at the front: 'Fortnum & Mason's Fresh Cod Roes and Preserved Ham, Chicken in Jelly, Whole Roast Pheasant, various soups: very rich Turtle Soup last night when I returned with the convoy at midnight.' And any officer, with loving and generous relations or not, was likely to fare particularly well at the high seasons of the years. On Christmas Day 1916, Captain Harry Yoxall, 18th Battalion King's Royal Rifle Corps, noted in his diary:

> At seven-thirty we had our Christmas dinner. The Menu was as follows:
>
> Tomato Soup
>
> Curried Prawns
>
> Roast Turkey & Sausages
> Roast & Mashed Potatoes
>
> Christmas Pudding   Minced Pies
> Devonshire Cream   Rum Butter
> Scotch Woodcock on Toast
>
> Cheese   Caviare
> Apples   Oranges   Tangerines   Almonds & Raisins   Nuts
> Candied Fruit   Chocolate

Coffee

———

Veuve Cliquot 1906
Whiskey   Rum
Port
Liqueur Brandy 1891
Rum Punch

With crackers and everything. Oh! to be in service now the food controller's here. Three courses only for soldiers in Blighty. But I'd give a good deal to be in Blighty all the same. Lord, how I'm getting weary of this war.

By contrast, an ordinary soldier might be lucky to receive a very modest reminder of the arrival of the Christmas season. Corporal James Brown Gingell, Royal Engineers, for example:

Xmas Day, day off. Not much to do, we only had our ordinary rations with the exception of a bit of Xmas pudding.

Such gargantuan meals as those referred to by Captain Yoxall were not easy to prepare in the conditions of the trenches. Private Jack Sweeney, 1st Battalion Lincolnshire Regiment, was for much of his time on the Western Front an officers' cook: the picture he paints shows the other side of this glittering coin:

17th Decr 1915
My luck is in — I have the employment of officers' cook again but it is not such a nice time as I had before as I have to go into the trenches and cook for them there, but it is better than doing sentry duty. It is very hard cooking on an old pail with coke, and the officers expect five course dinners just the same — well I do my best for them and I have suited them very well up to now.

Little allowance, however, was made for the often atrocious conditions:

Last time we were going into the trenches I had a terrible lot of goods to carry — all the tinned food the officers buy and I could hardly manage the lot but I had to get there somehow. There was myself and four other officers servants, and it was so dark we could not see our hands before us. We were going along a communication trench known as 'Lovers Walk' — I can hardly tell you for laughing but I did not laugh when I went into the water — it covered me and I lost the bag of food, but my mates managed to get me out. I did swear, my Word, I called Fritz everything. Afterwards we went on and then two of my mates fell in. It was a game and also a very cold bath. I arrived in the firing trench at last, then the officers wanted their dinner cooked. They saw the state I was in and only laughed — my face was all mud and I had lost my cap. I was in a state: it is a good job I am used to it.

33   *Regimental cook, Ancre Valley, 1916, photographed in cheerful mood, clearly not encountering some of the hazards described in this chapter by Private Sweeney. (Q1581)*

Private Sweeney's expertise as a cook was also appreciated by his comrades:

> I have a nice dugout where I cook and after the officers have had their dinner
> I let as many of the boys who are not on duty come in and have a warm and I
> make them a drop of hot tea, the officers get plenty of food, they waste a lot
> but the boys are glad to eat all they leave. The boys are so happy when they can
> have a warm and makes me feel happy to be able to give them a little comfort
> — you should see the steam rising off their clothing it is the only way they can
> get their clothes dry.

One other humble but vital aspect of trench life must be mentioned: not a subject much dealt with in letters and diaries, but still considered worthy of reference by some soldiers.

> The sanitary arrangements usually consisted of a pit, or series of pits, perhaps
> approached by a short trench and equipped with buckets or large biscuit tins
> which were emptied at night by the company 'pioneer'. The whole place was

34   A flooded dugout; the sergeant is being cheerful for the camera but such conditions could be dangerous. Prolonged occupation of flooded trenches could cause 'trench feet'. An RAMC sergeant, Harry Roberts, described what that meant: 'Your feet swell up and go completely dead. You could stick a bayonet into them and not feel a thing. If you are fortunate enough not to lose your feet and the swelling begins to go down, it is then that the agony begins. I have heard men cry and even scream with the pain and many had to have their feet and legs amputated.' (Q4665)

liberally treated with chloride of lime which provided a never-to-be-forgotten smell associated with trench life.

Private Harold Horne, 6th Bn Northumberland Fusiliers

Latrines were always dangerous places because of the regularity with which they had to be used. Jerry soon came to spot such places, and believe me, they were not places in which to linger.

Private Archie Surfleet, 13th Bn East Yorkshire Regt

Every army, as Napoleon said, marches on its stomach. When an army is not marching, but standing still in holes in the ground, it is likely to have obsessions about other things than the source of its next meal: for example about the weather. In fine, dry conditions life could be tolerable, but the Western Front was particularly vulnerable to the depredations of the rain. Rain damped spirits as well as uniforms. It soaked men to the skin in circumstances in which it was virtually impossible to dry out. It helped to induce that

35   *An Australian officer (probably the official Australian historian, C.E.W. Bean) wading through mud at Gueudecourt, Somme, December 1916. Mud was one of the wearying constants of trench life. Private Jack Sweeney wrote to his fiancée some weeks earlier: 'I will tell you just one little thing that happened to me on the Somme in the early hours of 14th Septr. I was wet to the skin, no overcoat, no water sheet, I had about 3 inches of clay clinging to my clothes and it was cold. I was in an open dug-out and do you know what I did — I sat down in the mud and cried. I do not think I have cried like that since I was a child.'*
(E(AUS) 572)

36   *Mud created problems for the gunner as well as the infantryman. A group of artillerymen attempt with a combination of shovels, strips of corrugated iron, onlookers' advice and sheer muscle power to bring an 18-pounder back on to dry land; Zillebeke, Ypres Salient, 9 August 1917. (Q6224)*

painful condition from which so many men suffered known as 'trench feet'. It was so disagreeable a component of trench life that it seemed to be always there.

Private Kenneth Garry wrote to his mother in January 1916, in the account quoted at the beginning of this chapter: 'It need not be said that it was raining: in fact it will save a lot of time in this chronicle if you assume that it is always raining except when otherwise stated.'

Captain Harry Yoxall, writing home in January 1917, put the same point with the aid of Shakespeare:

> Dearest Mater,
> With a hey-ho, the wind and the rain,
> The rain it raineth every day
> Except when it's snowing!

But it was what rain did to the ground that made it such a key participant in this stalemate war. It turned battlefields into quagmires and even firmly constructed trenches

37   *A reminder that more transport was drawn by horses than by the internal combustion engine in the Great War. Official figures state that 484,143 animals were killed or died in service with British forces. Captain Harry Yoxall spoke for many when he wrote 'It seems such a shame to drag animals into the mess we've made of things'. (Q5943)*

into alleyways of slippery, treacherous mud. In some sectors men compared the mud it produced to caramel; in others it laced the battle zones with muddy lakes and pools into which it was all too easy for men and horses to slide and fall. Once in, it was almost impossible to get out unaided; and many men lost their lives in the mud of the Western Front. It was a pathetic way to fall for one's country.

Private Tom Macdonald was in the Ypres Salient in early 1916:

> The Salient in winter was like Dante's Inferno. Shell holes full of slime, mud everywhere. Many men were wounded and trying to get back to Dressing Stations slipped in holes and were drowned. The Menin Road up to the Salient from Ypres they reckon claimed 900 a month.

The trenches in the chalk uplands of the Somme survived slightly better than those in low-lying Belgium, but even here conditions could be all but impossible after rain:

We left those Mericourt trenches yesterday. It was a pretty wood but the trenches were very wet in the rain and crumbled in a good deal — in fact in the relief two men had to be dragged out of the slush by force from above, so hopelessly did they get stuck up to their thighs in sucking sloppy mud.

Second Lieutenant Kenneth Macardle, 17th Bn Manchester Regt

There was something about the rain of this part of north-west Europe that seemed to give it a special malignance. Lance-Corporal Roland Mountfort, 10th Battalion Royal Fusiliers, described in a letter home a spell in new trenches in February 1916:

The weather kept fine for a day and then broke. It rained for two nights and on the third, between 3 and 6 a.m. it surpassed itself. It blew great guns, it snowed till the wet ground was covered 3in deep; it rained again and washed it away; sleet fell and froze as it fell; it rained again and washed that away. In the morning the trenches fell about our ears.

At the end of four days they relieved us and we waded out knee deep as of old. We struggled out somehow and crawled to a village about three miles back, the rain still coming down in BUCKETSFULL.

Perhaps not surprisingly Roland Mountfort's letter began with the statement: 'I don't like writing other than cheerful letters, but if I could compose one now I should be one of the most deserving VC heroes of the war.'

It has been raining here every day this week which makes things very uncomfortable, heaps of mud and lice including rats of course, but getting quite used to same now, my skin is quite raw owing to keeping on rubbing myself, haven't had a chance of getting water to wash a shirt out but hope to do something towards comfort tomorrow.

So wrote Private A.H. Hubbard, London Scottish, from the Somme front in May 1916, putting into one sentence all the major natural scourges of trench life. Lice and rats became an inevitable, unforgettable component of service in the line. Almost everyone was lousy. As one subaltern, Second Lieutenant James Dale, 2nd Battalion Liverpool Scottish, put it: 'I have become a base depot for sundry lesser fauna who crawl and bite.'

Lice — or 'chats', as they were often called — got into clothes and once there were virtually immovable. Men ran lighted matches up the seams of shirts and enjoyed the crackle of incinerated livestock, but this, though it afforded sweet revenge, was only a temporary sweeping back of the tide:

If you're nearly frozen, they keep quiet: as soon as you warm up those blasted lice start to bite like the devil. It's horrible. I often think it is one of the worst things we have to endure out here.

Private Archie Surfleet, 13th Bn East Yorkshire Regt

I had a lice hunt this forenoon and oh my I caught thousands quite big fat ones — and wee fellows — they get into the folds of your kilt, down the seams of your shirt the devils, how they get there I don't know — nothing kills them — powders etc. have no effect — the only way is to heave a few Rum Jars at them. ['Rum-jars' was soldiers' slang for German trench mortar bombs!]

Private Peter McGregor, 14th Bn Argyle and Sutherland Highlanders

And then there were the rats.

There are millions!! Some are huge fellows, nearly as big as cats. Several of our men were awakened to find a rat snuggling down under the blanket alongside them!

Major Walter Vignoles

There are the greatest old rats in the trenches that you ever saw. They are so tame they won't run away but just toddle along in front of you just out of reach. One of our men went up to one the other day and kicked it like a football.

Second Lieutenant Geoffrey Lillywhite

Where the rats came from was a mystery. Good regiments like ours kept their trenches clean and tidy, so far as they could, and the only unwelcome smell was the salutary if unpleasant one of chloride of lime in all the appropriate places. But they were everywhere. There was one old fellow who was quite well known in our sector. I met him one day in a communication trench. He could walk on top of the mud into which I sunk at every step.

He was enormous, with ferocious and venomous eyes, and I freely admit I flattened myself against the trench wall and let him go past, which he did without turning his head.

Lieutenant Cyril Drummond, 135th Battery Royal Field Artillery

Whilst asleep during the night we were frequently awakened by rats running over us. When this happened too often for my liking I would lie on my back and wait for a rat to linger on my legs, then violently heave my legs upwards, throwing the rat into the air; occasionally I would hear a grunt when the rat landed on a fellow victim.

Driver R. L. Venables

In one of the dugouts the other night, two men were smoking by the light of the candle, very quiet. All at once candle moved and flickered. Looking up they saw a rat was dragging it away — fact. Another: very quiet and saw rat washing itself like a cat just behind the candle. Some as big as rabbits. I was in the trench the other night and one jumped over the parapet. Made sure it was a German's head looking over, so kept still and watched, and found it was a rat.

Private Frank Bass

7 'Keep the Hun on his toes'

Mud and vermin were the lesser enemies in this war; the real enemy was the human one, a matter of yards away, in his own muddy, rat-infested trenches.

> At night we would be on sentry, head and shoulders above the trench gazing into No Man's Land, which was lines of tangled barbed wire in front of ours and also in front of the Germans. Only yards at times separated us. In fact so close you could hear a chap coughing.
>
> *Private Tom MacDonald, 9th Bn Royal Sussex Regt*

Variously known as Jerry, Fritz, the Hun, the Boche — Boche (also spelt Bosche or Bosch) was French slang for 'German' — it was the German whom Tommy had come to fight, outwit and kill. Launched by 'Kaiser Bill' into unprovoked attack in 1914, he had seized territories that were not his own. The purpose of trench warfare as far as the British were concerned was, initially, to prevent him from seizing any more: ultimately, to send him packing to Berlin; and, in the meantime, to hound and harass him with every conceivable ruse or device.

There were times and places where the French were content to 'live and let live'. Even the Germans were happy at times to follow this philosophy. But for the British this was merely playing at war. They favoured the doctrine of the offensive: there must be continual raids on the enemy lines to seize prisoners and cause casualties; there must be regular 'strafes' by the artillery; it must be the aim of the British battalions to dominate No Man's Land, to justify the claim that 'the German wire is our front line'. In official terms, time in the trenches was to be 'utilized not for passive defence but for exhausting the enemy's troops'. The Hun must be kept on his toes.

In 1915, Private Harold Horne and his comrades of the 6th Battalion of the Northumberland Fusiliers moved south from the Ypres Salient, 'where the trenches were fifteen yards apart and we and "Jerry" could call to each other', to Messines:

> Things had been quiet there for some time and the trenches were clean and tidy and dry with fields of poppies behind us and in front of us in No Man's Land which was three or four hundred yards across. When we took over this sector our Brigadier told us that the trenches were like a garden but as we were soldiers and not 'bloody gardeners' we had to liven things up.

The night hours, inevitably, were the time chosen for putting into practice the philosophy

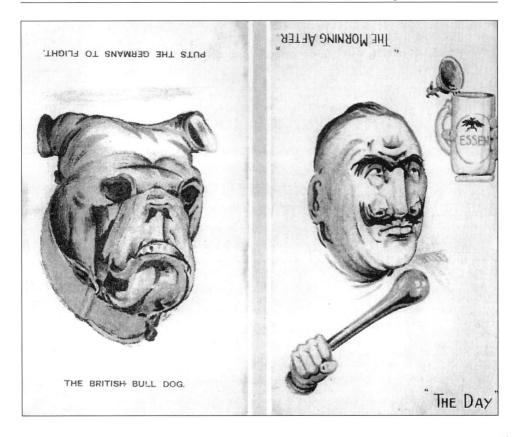

THE BRITISH BULL DOG.

PUTS THE GERMANS TO FLIGHT.

" THE MORNING AFTER "

" THE DAY "

38   The enemy cartooned. Such cards — to be turned upside down to get their message — could be bought by the Tommy in France. 'The Day' — 'Der Tag' — was reputed to be a favourite pre-war toast in German military circles: it was held to be convincing evidence of a long-held intention to go to war. (Mr Malcolm Greenhill)

of the High Command. The 'free firework displays' often referred to by the Tommy were an essential component of this nocturnal activity, as in each front line sentries peered through the unnatural glow of flares and Very lights to see if they could make out what the enemy was doing. For men out in No Man's Land, whether carrying out a reconnaissance or a raid or, more humbly, engaged in such routines as the repairing of the barbed wire defences, the sudden illumination of this dangerous zone could be extremely unnerving.

> Very lights were trying, it is so natural to want to duck as these terrors of the working party streak upwards, but our platoon sergeant told us to remain motionless. And what a sight it was over the top in the sickly glare of those lights. Everything seemed to stand out: the barbed wire, the posts, the shell-holes — all bare and desolate, a spectacle of utter devastation.
>
> *Private Archie Surfleet, 13th Bn East Yorkshire Regt*

39 Young German soldiers in cheerful mood wearing 'pickelhaube' helmets. (Mr. A. L. Atkins)

Perhaps those most able to take in the unique atmosphere of No Man's Land were men pushed out into listening posts between the lines. Rifleman A.H. Young, 1/18th London Regiment, London Irish Rifles, went out to one at Givenchy in May 1915:

> We could hear the Germans talking quite plainly. It was a curious experience listening to our own and German bullets whistling overhead and to be right in the centre of things, as it were. The only company I had besides my companion, was the dead piled all around, Germans, British and Indians, and the odour is indescribable, especially as a lot of the 23rd were lying there who had only recently been killed.

The philosophy of the offensive has been much argued about. It has been claimed that its losses outweighed its gains, that, because of the inevitable casualties, it drained good and energetic battalions of their most enterprising officers and men, that it inspired COs

40   *The Tommy who found this
     picture captioned it: 'German
     machine gun mounted for
     Anti-Aircraft. The man on
     the right is an NCO.'
     (Mr A.L. Atkins)*

to launch acts of bravado to provide worthwhile entries for the battalion diary and evidence of keenness for their superiors. The defenders of the philosophy assert that it kept the British as well as the Germans on their toes, that as well as wearing down the enemy it trained and honed Britain's largely amateur army for the set-piece battles that were bound to come in the fullness of time. As for those who had to carry out the doctrine in practice, many loathed and feared the whole business, but others found in it a remarkable personal fulfilment.

For Lieutenant W.T. Colyer (formerly Private Colyer of the Artists' Rifles and now a junior officer in the 2nd Battalion Royal Dublin Fusiliers) this was what trench war was about. In April 1915 he found himself covering for a working party in No Man's Land:

> How different it feels to be doing something! Back there in the trenches I feel like a rat in a trap, because I can't move out of it, however many shells they send over, and can do nothing in my own defence. Here, though a hundred yards nearer the Boche and quite exposed, I feel pretty much as if I were walking down the back garden at home. I don't feel any more frightened of Fritz than if I were playing hide-and-seek in the dark with him. Kingsley is severely critical of what he evidently regards as my foolhardiness in wandering about in such a brazen

way while so close to the enemy lines. For something to do I visit each one of my men and ask him if he has observed or heard anything of interest. I know jolly well he hasn't, beforehand; for if he had I should have noticed it myself. Still, an occasional question helps to keep them on the alert.

Second Lieutenant Kenneth Macardle, 17th Battalion Manchester Regiment, was another young subaltern who found exultation and satisfaction in these nocturnal war games. He confided to his diary in May 1916:

> I love being out of trenches and searching for adventure in No Man's Land at night . . . Now that Carter has gone home on special leave I have to go out every night myself. They try to pamper me — expect me to suffer from nervous strain but I don't. I have breakfast in bed and sleep again; I live in HQ in great luxury and sometimes when I am out on a fighting patrol, the Colonel sits up for me!!

Patrolling at night was an acquired craft: taking greenhorns out 'in search of adventure' could produce strange results. Macardle was out with 25 men on the Somme front in May 1916 when unexpectedly a white mist came down. Some of the men began 'to see things':

> A message was sent up to me from one that we had a Hun cornered and would I surround him. We converged with lowered bayonets upon the prostrate form lying in the grass — a fallen log. But it had raised a fatal ripple of excitement — too much for the untrained men from the company — two of them suddenly shot away, ran fiercely into the mist and plunged their bayonets into a very obvious hummock of grass. Then a message reached me that a patrol was approaching through the fog. My own Corporal came up and said the Company was all windy and overstrained — one can't patrol dangerous land with men like that — they are apt to loose off at the man in front; so I took them home.

But even after this curious outing there was a moment of warm satisfaction when they returned to their trenches, with the sense of a dangerous exploit boldly undertaken and a companionship shared. 'We sat in the light of two candles and smoked — everybody smoked: the great calm and good humour of these occasions settled down on me.' Sadly this brilliant young officer was killed in No Man's Land some weeks later shortly after the beginning of the Battle of the Somme. Indeed, perhaps not unexpectedly, some of the best accounts of daring raids into No Man's Land are to be found in the accounts of young men who did not survive. The following is taken from a letter to his mother by Second Lieutenant Ian Melhuish, 7th Battalion Somerset Light Infantry, written on 21 October 1915, just six days before he was killed when on a later patrol:

> Whilst in the trenches I had to take out 2 Patrols: my object both times was to capture a Boche alive. The first time I took 3 men with me, but one only cared

about coming all the way with me. We went right up to their barbed wire and located a working party. We could also hear the Huns talking. There was no one however to capture. We crawled about in the grass from 6 p.m. to 2 a.m. and then made our way home.

The second night I took out 2 men whom I could trust and this time located a listening post from which they were sending up flares. Unfortunately the sentries caught sight of us and turned some machine guns on to us. We lay v. still in the grass and after some time they thought we had either gone away or been killed, for they only fired now and then. Then a thick fog began to develop and we were able to creep quite close to the wire of the post and throw in 3 bombs, all of which failed to explode. (These bombs are v. terrible if they do explode and they blow everything near them to pieces.) Well, after the bombs had been thrown we bolted for a ditch and remained there till after they had finished searching for us with rapid fire, when we returned home.

The worst part was that the Boche had succeeded in killing and wounding two of our men in the trenches with bullets aimed at us.

If raids which succeeded produced their own satisfaction, raids which failed did not. In May 1916 Private Jack Sweeney wrote in a letter to his fiancée:

It is simply murder at this part of the line. There is one of our officers hanging on the German barbed wire and a lot of attempts have been made to get him and a lot of brave men have lost their lives in the attempt. The Germans know that we are sure to try and get him in so all they have to do is to put two or three fixed rifles on to him and fire every few seconds — he must be riddled with bullets by now: he was leading a bombing party one night and got fixed in the wire — the raid was a failure.

Lance-Sergeant Elmer Cotton, 5th Battalion Northumberland Fusiliers, described the tragic loss of another young officer in his notebook in August 1915:

We were in no. 78 trench — the Germans had built a dummy hedge and it was necessary to find the reason why. Accordingly on the night of the 23rd Lt Winkworth, Sgt Coppick and Pte Longworth left our trench, word was passed down the line and all firing ceased, no flare lights were put up from our trenches. They would normally be out about½ an hour but an hour passed and they had not returned. I was Sgt of the line from 9 to 12 midnight and at 11 p.m. I became anxious and was about to send out a search party when a sentry in a bay challenged a figure in front of his trench. It was Pte Longworth and he came in minus his hat or rifle and with a revolver in his hand. He reported the Lt shot and lying between the lines in 'no man's land'. The Captain, myself and 5 bearers then went out to his aid. We stumbled through our own barbed wire and then along a hedge, fell down an old trench and finally found the brave officer with the Sgt who had already carried him about 50 yards from the

41   A raiding party of the 10th Scottish Rifles heading into No Man's Land, near Arras, 24 March 1917. Most raids were carried out by night, but in certain circumstances, usually after an intensive bombardment intended to cow resistance in the enemy trenches, raids were carried out by day. This one was even more remarkable because of the presence of an official photographer. (Q5102)

dummy hedge towards our line. He said they had crawled up to the hedge and the Lt had raised himself up to see better but they had been seen and a machine gun sprayed them with bullets, one hitting Lt Winkworth in the elbow and passing into his stomach. We got him onto a stretcher, gave him 2 grains of morphine and carried him safely back to our own trenches. One or two bullets were fired at us but we got back safely. The brave Lieutenant, who though a newcomer promised to become a very good officer, died the next day.

Deaths at the hands of the enemy were expected; deaths of comrades by bullets from one's own side made men angry and bitter. Yet in the darkness of the trenches, with all the possibilities of confusion, misunderstanding and panic that inevitably existed in this dangerous twilight world, such deaths were not uncommon. Private Archie Surfleet's battalion, the 13th East Yorkshires, was about to pull out of the line when, on its last night:

One of our Sergeants went out on patrol just in front of our line. They had done the job and were coming in when, owing to a misunderstanding over the password, our company Lewis gunners opened fire, killing the sergeant and two men. They had got no reply to their challenge; raids by the enemy were very frequent then so, fearing an attack, they thought to do their duty by opening fire on the supposed raiders. The dreadful pity of it is that today I have been told that this damned good soldier, the sergeant in charge (who had been out here since 1914) was somewhat hard of hearing and it seems almost certain that he failed to hear the challenge. This most regrettable incident has cast a gloom over the whole Battalion: it has taken what little wind was left clean out of our sails.

Captain R.S. Cockburn took part in a raid which ended in a somewhat similar disaster, though here the cause was the failure of the appropriate officer in Cockburn's battalion, the 10th King's Royal Rifles, to inform the battalion next in line that the raid was to happen. Men in that battalion's listening post opened up and Cockburn's NCO, Corporal Hadley, fell at his feet. Cockburn stood up and shouted in the darkness:

'Stop that firing! We're the 10th KRR.'
  When I turned to look at the still figure on the ground, I knew that Corporal Hadley had been shot. I caught hold of him under the arms, and the other man with me, Smith, took his legs; we carried him with some difficulty back to our own sap, and sent for a stretcher bearer. But it was too late, as Corporal Hadley was already dead. He had been shot through the head and must have been killed instantly — a very brave and upright man who was never replaced.

The unhappy footnote to this story is that this particular escapade — the idea of which was to attack an enemy listening post — had been devised at the last moment by the Colonel because a previous scheme had been found to be impracticable. He had decided that he would 'think of something else to do that night'. Cockburn added the comment: 'In those days it was the commonest thing to carry out little operations like that for the sake of doing something, although their value might be questionable, and their risks not at all questionable.'
  'Our fellows hate the Boche like anything.' So wrote a young officer at the height of the Battle of the Somme. But many men had an enormous respect for the German as a fighting soldier, and it is on the whole remarkable how little animosity was felt for the men in field grey on the other side of the wire.

The Hun is a strange fellow. We are constantly gingering him up with raids and artillery shots. On the whole he fights very well against odds and I can't help admiring him. You can't think how deep an interest you feel in those people across there, separated from us only by that narrow strip of bog and those two entanglements of rusty wire. And somehow one doesn't — or at any rate I do not — feel much rancour. 'With malice towards none' . . . 'Forgive them, for they know not what they do' — and they do it jolly well. That is as far as the actual combatants are concerned; but we shall not forget the people who made the war.
  Captain Harry Yoxall, 18th Bn Kings Royal Rifle Corps

42 German prisoners being brought in on 1 July 1916. The curiosity of the Tommies watching is
understandable. It was rare for even front line soldiers actually to see the enemy. (Q30)

I was shocked to hear that Tom had been wounded. One thinks that I would
feel anger, burning anger, against the Germans. Not so! The whole damned
show is so impersonal that one cannot (at least I cannot) feel any personal
emotion (except, perhaps, fear) when in the thick of things. Hope, revenge,
anger, contempt — any of these would be a sustaining emotion in action, but
very few experience them, I believe.

Sapper Garfield Powell, Royal Engineers

Pity, too, was another emotion which the Tommy could feel in certain circumstances.
Having watched a group of prisoners being brought in on the first day of the Somme
battle, Gunner Hiram Sturdy noted:

They were not big savage hulks of men with bristling whiskers or criminal
foreheads. They were young men, bandaged and battered, a solid bunch of
nerves after having I expect been through a hellish bombardment. The most
savage comment I heard while watching the prisoners came from an
infantryman. That was 'Poor buggers!' It makes one feel glad to belong to a

43   A cigarette after a fight. Canadian and German wounded pausing for a smoke before
proceeding to a dressing station. Battle of Passchendaele, 6 October 1917. (CO2212)

fighting force where 'poor buggers' is said about enemy prisoners. Fancy seeing
it in print in the morning newspapers: 'Our infantrymen are sorry for the
enemy prisoners and wonder why he has to kill them.' Those who printed it
would be on parade next day.

The enemy was, however, indisputably there to be wounded and killed. The whole
purpose of all those months of cheerful manly training in rifle and bayonet drill was that
eventually a German would be in the sight of one's rifle or vulnerable to the exultation of
a bayonet charge. In practice it was not always so simple. Sapper Garfield Powell, just
quoted, was trained to disable and kill by gas. He commented in his diary in June 1916:
'What a difference there is between the war of visions and the actual thing. In a few days
we go up to let off the gas. More dirty work or rather more help towards the triumph of
Right over Might.' Gas, however, was impersonal. Killing with bullet or bayonet made
one acutely aware of the human being whose life one was taking.

Private Jack Sweeney killed two Germans during a trench raid on the British lines in
the small hours of 21 November 1916. He was in a dugout with two other officers'
servants when the raid began after a flurry of shells and shouting:

They began to throw bombs down into the dugout but we were safe as long as we kept clear of the stairs. Presently I heard someone coming down the stairs — I shouted 'Who are you?' — he said something but I pulled my trigger and he said no more, he rolled down to me with two men very much alive following him up. I let go at them, one I killed, the other died later, the other two servants shot five, and one was wounded. The German that I shot who died afterwards was a fine looking man. I was there when he died, poor chap — I did feel sorry but it was my life or his, he was speaking but none of us could understand a word he said, to tell you the truth I had a tear myself — I thought to myself perhaps he has a Mother or Dad also a sweetheart and a lot of things like that. I was really sorry I did it but God knows I could not help myself.

Lieutenant R.A. Chell, 10th Battalion Essex Regiment, killed his first enemy in September 1915 at Mametz on the Somme. He spotted a bulletproof sniper's plate on the other side of a newly created crater some 70 yards away:

After about fifteen minutes quiet watching — with my rifle in a ready position — I saw a capless bald head come up behind the plate. The day was bright and clear and I hadn't the slightest difficulty in taking a most deliberate aim at the very centre of that bright and shiny pate — but somehow I couldn't press the trigger: to shoot such a 'sitter' so deliberately in cold blood required more moral courage than I possessed. After a good look round he went down and I argued with myself about my duty. My bald-headed opponent had been given a very sporting chance and if he were fool enough to come up again I must shoot him unflinchingly. I considered it my duty to be absolutely ready for that contingency. After about two minutes he came up again with added boldness and I just did my duty. I had been a marksman before the war and so had no doubt about the instantaneousness of that man's death: aim and trigger pressure were as deliberate as when I'd been grouping at 100 yards at test ranges in 1913 and 1914 and that bald head was a perfect target. Still, I felt funny for days and the shooting of another German at 'stand-to' the next morning did nothing to remove those horrid feelings I had.

Of course there were those who killed without hesitation and with relish, but even zealous campaigners could hesitate when they found an enemy entirely at their mercy. Thus one enthusiastic 'thrusting' officer much quoted in this book, the Coldstream Guards lieutenant Alex Wilkinson, could write of an attack in the very last days of the war in 1918: 'I had sworn to shoot the first Hun I saw, but I could not bring myself to do it' (See Chapter 16). Killing at a distance, by artillery or machine-gun fire was a different matter: distant targets did not so obviously declare their humanity. But killing in close-up required a formidable commitment from which many shied away. Thus another soldier of the Coldstream Guards much quoted by me elsewhere could find satisfaction when the war ended in the fact that he had never knowingly taken a German life.[1] Advance, seize ground, take prisoners, yes; but it was not always necessary to blast an enemy into eternity in order to win a battle or win a war.

Yet against that it has to be acknowledged that killing, and the belief in the need to kill, was central to the infantryman's culture. Plunging bayonets into sacks to the accompaniment of blood-curdling yells was not just fun and games at training camps, it was intended to make it seem equally easy to plunge bayonets into men. 'Blood-lust' was deliberately taught and reinforced by 'doping the minds of all with propagandic poison'. So wrote the thrusting commander par excellence Brigadier-General F.P. Crozier, who believed that in the matter for hyping a soldier for action there were no holds barred:

> The German atrocities (many of which I doubt in secret), the employment of gas in action, the violation of French women, and the 'official murder' of Nurse Cavell all help to bring out the brute-like bestiality which is so necessary for victory . . . The British soldier is a kindly fellow and it is safe to say, despite the dope, seldom oversteps the mark of barbaric propriety in France, save occasionally to kill prisoners he cannot be bothered to escort back to his lines.
>
> In order that he shall enter into the true spirit of the show, however, the fun of the fair as we may call it, it is necessary to corrode his mentality with bitter-sweet vice and to keep him up to the vicious scratch on all occasions . . . It is the only way in war, and both sides follow it.[2]

Though there were many who jibbed at such a code, there were undoubtedly many others who did not.

[1] F.E. Noakes in *The Imperial War Museum Book of 1918: Year of Victory*, Sidgwick & Jackson 1998

[2] Brigadier F.P. Crozier, *A Brass-Hat in No Man's Land*. Jonathon Cape, 1930, pp. 42-2

8 'Out on rest'

After its allotted period in the front line, a battalion would move back to reserve trenches. The normal pattern was four days in followed by four days out, but, as Private Henry Bolton put it, 'you must not think those four days were spent lounging about'. (His diary entry continued: 'You could often hear the remark "I would rather be in the firing line" and more than once have I passed that remark myself.') At the very least there were fatigues, which often included exhausting trips up to the front with supplies. At the most there were operations of very considerable danger. Private Edgar Foreman, 1/15th Battalion London Regiment (generally known as the Civil Service Rifles), described a particularly hazardous assignment in a letter home written in September 1915:

> When we were in reserve our whole Company had to form a covering party to another Battalion, who came up to dig a new fire-trench at night-time. As soon as it was dark we went out in front until we were midway between the German and English trenches, where we lay down at about 20 paces interval between each pair of us: the first night we were by ourselves at 10 paces. Our job was to form a screen so that the working party could not be surprised. We were there from 8 until 2 a.m. The first night was the most exciting, the Germans shelling our trenches and our artillery replying; we could hear the pieces from the shrapnel dropping all round us and a large number of stray shots whizzing through the long grass, it was the longest six hours I have ever spent, but the only casualties in our party were an officer and a private who were shot by our own men mistaking them for Germans; they were both killed.

By the time this task was completed, there had been more deaths, including several fatalities caused by that formidable German weapon, the *Minenwerfer*, unaffectionately known as 'Minnie':

> a contrivance the Germans have which can throw a bomb 200 pounds in weight and 5ft long a distance of 1000 yards, it explodes like a mine and kills by concussion. They sent several over every day and killed a good many. One of the four men of our Battalion who were killed that way I knew quite well, he was the last of five brothers all of whom have been killed in the war.

The reputation of this weapon was fully justified; the Germans were well ahead of the Allies in the use of trench mortars. They had 150 *Minenwerfer* available when the war began and they were precision pieces very effective in trench fighting.

44   *Anzac troops washing the mud off their waders after a spell in the trenches, January 1917. (E(AUS) 120)*

Normally, however, reserve trenches meant hard rather than risky work, to be borne with weary resignation, or, as in the case of this 16-year-old, Private Frank Birkinshaw, Royal Warwickshire Regiment, writing home in May 1915, with breezy if cynical good humour:

> We are relieved tonight and go back for four days rest. I think it must be a little joke to call it rest, for we do twice as much work as in the trenches. Every night we 'man' the reserve trenches until two o'clock in the morning. After that we lie in the woods until six o'clock: then we march back, sleep, eat, have rifle inspection and wonder why we ever joined the army: until six o'clock at night when the same thing happens again. In our spare time we go and mend roads or pick up jam tins which other regiments have left behind.

But sooner or later the moment would arrive when the battalion would withdraw to rest billets well clear of the battle zone:

> There was no more delightful sensation in those days, than marching on a good hard road under a bright moon to rest billets far behind the line. You were

45   *An unusual billet behind the line: Canadian soldiers occupying a ruined barn at Villers-au-Bois, June 1917. (CO 2076)*

so glad to be away from the shells: you could look forward to sleeping in a bed, perhaps between sheets; you knew that you might, if it was summer time, procure fresh eggs and milk and vegetables; you might wear your soft cap again, instead of the steel helmet which was such a fearful weight. Your peace of mind was only interrupted by thoughts of what the Battalion was, when it last came out for a rest.

Captain R.S. Cockburn, 10th King's Royal Rifle Corps

Perhaps most important of all at such times was the reassurance both to the eye and the ear that there was another world still continuing only a matter of miles from the zone of barbed wire and devastation from which they had just emerged:

After lying in holes in the earth, sometimes waterlogged, wet through to the skin, it was delightful to arrive in a town without war scars, even though the women moved about like sacks of potatoes tied around the middle. Nevertheless their feminine voices were pleasant to the ear, after those of strident sergeant-majors and their kin, linked as they were to the discordance of bursting shells.

Private W. Carson Catron, Hull Commercials

For men being relieved after a hard spell in the trenches a slog of several miles with heavy kit was a tough beginning to their time of rest, but, as Private Henry Bolton, 1st Battalion East Surrey Regiment, wrote after such a march:

We were well repaid for our walk, for Locre was a beautiful place with a grand old church and it had not been shelled. The first morning I was there was Sunday and the bells of the fine old church rang out their welcome and the Belgian people (of course mostly ladies or very aged men) flocked to their call dressed in their best and it made one think of Dear old Home and the Loved ones we had left behind.

This was a time when trench-hardened soldiers found supreme satisfaction in simple, ordinary things:

Imagine my feelings when I got onto a straw mattress that night! To be able to sit at a table and have a plate to eat your food from, well — it reminds you of once upon a time.

Private Albert Johnson, 11th Bn Royal West Kents

We don't need much, now, to make us happy: a pile of clean straw, a clean shirt, ten francs, an estaminet out of Jerry's range and we are as happy as sandboys.

Private Archie Surfleet, 13th Bn East Yorkshire Regt

To be clean again, not to be lousy, to feel for a while like a decent human being — these were among the best pleasures of being away from the trenches. The Army recognized this need and had its own special rituals to provide for it. Private Edgar Foreman described the experience of getting cleaned up, army style, in a letter of November 1915:

> We got a hot bath in on the Sunday morning, it was one of the best organized things I have yet seen in the army. They *do* you in batches of 12 (I had the luck to be in the first 12). You first of all throw all your clothing into a trough under your own number (1 to 12), it is taken in charge by an RAMC man, who only deals with your special number, the underclothing is changed and the khaki brushed and the seams ironed. While this is being done you are allowed five minutes in a tub of hot water. (The twelve men soaking in twelve steaming tubs would be a good photo for the *Daily Mirror.*) When you are turned out for the next lot to get, you go to another trough to find clean underclothing and your brushed khaki all ready for you.

(Unhappily this was Private Foreman's last letter home; he was killed by a shell together with two others of his battalion on 10 November 1915, the day after this letter was written.)

Others, however, found the Army's bath-house routine much less organized and a good deal less satisfactory. Private Archie Surfleet and his comrades of the 13th Battalion of the East Yorkshire Regiment, for example, in February 1917:

> We marched to the bath-house (the usual converted brewery) and stripped in an outhouse. The bathroom was a large, bare place, floored with duck-boards, the sort used in the trenches, and we trooped in, standing in lines like so many shivering jellies, for the boards were covered in ice. Then after the usual wait, with much spluttering of air in the pipes, a thin stream of scalding hot water shot down on us. Note that: stood on ice — scalding hot water on your head! It struck me as a likely idea for the next Spanish Inquisition. I wonder we did not drop dead from shock, but after the scramble for your togs, out we went into the snow!

Gone too along with the individual bath-tubs was the scrupulous laundering of individual uniforms of the kind that had delighted Private Foreman in 1915. As the Army grew in size and complexity, there was less time for such civilized niceties. Now when dirty, lice-infested shirts were discarded at the bath-house, it was anybody's guess whose allegedly clean shirt you were issued with as you left. Private Archie Surfleet voiced a common reaction when he wrote in his diary in July 1916:

> Speaking of 'chats', lots of the lads say they prefer to 'keep their own' — which sounds a pretty damnable comment to be forced to make, though I tend to agree with the sentiment! How the hell they expect anyone to put on fresh shirts when they are already at least as lousy as those discarded beats me!

46   *Bath routine. Men of the 2nd Australian Battalion waiting outside a bath house at Ypres,*
      1 November 1917. (E(AUS) 1067)

Despite such drawbacks, time out from the trenches had its very special quality. Private Surfleet, summing up his whole experience as a soldier, wrote: 'I think the happiest times I had during the 1914 war were with the PBI when we were at rest in those pleasant villages like Saint-Venant, Robecq, Camblain-Chatelain and a few more.'

Among the 'few more' Private Surfleet did not name was the village of Longuevillette, where he spent a particularly happy time in January 1917 in spite of 'quite the coldest weather I have experienced':

> It is daylight now and a wonderful winter's day. When we are off duty, which is frequent, both officers and men spend most of the time sliding on the frozen pond: great fun on a really first-class slide. The old folks come out of their cottages and stand around while we dash about: they seem a bit surprised to see our officers mixing so readily with the men. (I must say our officers are very good sports.) I hope this life will continue.

A few days later he wrote again in the same vein:

> I have been waiting, half afraid, for something to put an end to this wonderful time and I suppose this has made me delay writing up my diary. It has been almost too good to be true and we are becoming so 'civilized' the keeping of a diary seems absurd.

Almost the supreme pleasure of being out on rest was simply 'taking it easy'. Sapper Garfield Powell wrote in his diary on a May day in 1916:

> Am writing these notes in a field at the back of the billet. Nearly all the section are here — sprawled out in the sun. One Elphick is trying to play a piccolo. Another — Jenkins G. E. (called Eddie, George, Ted, Ned and many other things, mostly bad) — is stripped to the waist and washing in a tin — evidently enjoying it. A few seconds ago he was looking carefully at his shirt — for diamonds? Davies D.J. is listening to Elphick talking (he has given up the piccolo to indulge in his usual pastime). The others are watching the sky — except myself, of course, who is writing (should it be 'who am' or 'who is'?).

Being British soldiers, it was inevitable that they should resort to traditional British sports; if the necessary equipment was not available, it could be invented. Lance-Corporal Roland Mountfort wrote in a letter of June 1916:

> Some enterprising person being possessed of a red tennis ball our latest recreations are tennis with entrenching tools on a hard court about as level as a rockery and cricket with the aid of a biscuit tin and a piece of packing case. After all I don't see why a monotonous dead level and faultlessly turned implements are necessary to sport. You get so many more variations from our method.

In fact the British affection for ball games was irrepressible. There is at least one authentic case of football being played on the Arras road between 4 a.m. and 5.30 a.m. on a September morning (according to Rifleman A.H. Young, London Irish Rifles, in his account 'My Experiences on the Western Front', written in 1915).

Inevitably, the tiny country villages of France and Belgium became well known to the Tommy and he to them and in particular it was to that peculiarly French — or Belgian — institution known as the estaminet to which many of them were drawn. The estaminet was not at all like a British public house, but it provided a similar service: it offered drink, company, a chance to let the hair down, and, for the persevering, a brief oblivion. Lance-Corporal Mountfort described the three estaminets which he and his fellow 10th Royal Fusiliers regularly visited as much of a muchness, both as to appearance or stock in trade.

> The latter consists almost entirely of a fearful thin beer sour as vinegar, vin rouge, vin blanc and cognac. The bar is in the front room and is merely a small dock, like a county court witness box, in one corner with a few shelves behind. I have not encountered an inhabitant who speaks English yet, but almost all of us know enough French to carry on an entente cordiale. English money is taken at the rate of 10 pence a franc; beer is two sous a glass and red wine 1 franc 75 a bottle. The latter is a sort of claret and not bad stuff.

But for those who found their satisfactions in these sparsely furnished, unsophisticated village drinking-houses, they could hold, at least in retrospect, a not unromantic glow.

Writing many years afterwards, W. Carson Catron, former Private in the Hull Commercials, put into his affectionate description of one representative estaminet the essence of many convivial evenings with his battalion comrades:

> Within the estaminet oil lamps shone dimly on a dozen or so beer drinkers seated around a large table. Smaller tables occupied the corners. Madame struggled to the large table with an outsize jug on the side of which were painted two flying angels. She poured the frothless, spineless fluid the jug contained into the empty glasses to the accompaniment of a bedlam of voices. She laughed as she poured, each time lightening the weight of her jug, meanwhile jerking out *'Oui Monsieur'* to all enquiries, regardless. The last glass filled, she rested the jug at her feet as dirty pieces of paper, like overworked blotting paper, were pushed around the table to her. She took them up, examined them, then placed them in her pocket, before collecting the metal coins some of the men were offering her. Finally, with a *'Merci beaucoup'*, she turned and hurried off to recharge the jug as quickly as her legs and her ample proportions would allow.
>
> Back in the room she watched those around the table hold up their charged glasses high. A voice called out, 'All set? Go!' Heads were thrown back, mouths opened wide and down it went, followed almost immediately by pandemonium. The last man to bang on the table had to pay for the next round. Madame stood by, hugging her replenished jug to her bosom awaiting instructions.

This kind of performance could have only one result where weaker heads were concerned. Tommies lurching back to their billets the worse for liquor were not uncommon sights on French roads:

> It was one day towards the end of March 1918: several of us were walking along the road towards St Omer. Perhaps two hundred yards away was a Tommy whose unsteady gait was unmistakable. As he drew slowly but surely nearer a young French peasant girl came abreast of us. She saw the Tommy even as we did and as she spotted that unmistakable gait she said, partly to herself, partly to our little group and partly to the universe at large *ANGLAIS SOLDATS BEAUCOUP ZIGZAG TOUS LES JOURS!'* 'Ziz-zag' himself drew near, then passed beyond us, talking to himself. That was all of sixty years ago but I can still see Tommy, and still hear the almost sad note in Ma'amselle's voice.
> *Private W. G. Brown, 2/3rd Field Ambulance, 59th (North Midland) Division*

It was, of course, while out on rest that the British Tommy and the French or Belgian civilian came into contact. The obvious question that must be asked is: how well did they get on together, thrust as they were into close proximity by the fortunes of war? In fact, this is an area where generalizations are difficult. Experiences varied widely. Some soldiers report favourably on their relations with the local people, others much less so. The evidence is, perhaps inevitably, somewhat contradictory. Sometimes, indeed, a soldier will write in one vein in one letter and in a totally opposite vein in another. Second Lieutenant Ian Melhuish, 7th Battalion Somerset Light Infantry, for example:

> It is v. nice here. The French people we come across are v. pleasant.
> *Letter of 26 July 1915*

> I am afraid the much-vaunted generosity of the French people is on the wane. They are not anxious to give much away, in fact their chief object seems to be to make as much as possible out of the British.
> *Letter of 11 August 1915*

Melhuish's second, sourer note was, it must be admitted, frequently struck by soldiers who felt that they had been less than justly treated by the local shopkeepers, aware that they had what would in modern terms be called a captive market. Second Lieutenant Arthur Gibbs was, for example, writing in August 1916:

> There is quite a big town near here where we dined last night. We did a little shopping and got some very nice fresh fruit, for which we were charged much too much. Some idiots at the beginning of the war spoilt all the shopkeepers, the result is that we are all robbed.

Or there is Private Jack Sweeney, writing home less legibly than usual in November 1915:

> I have just paid a Franck [sic] for this Rotten pencil, it is not worth a penny. The French people here do put the pence on to us, they rob us every way they can, there are not many English soldiers that will give them a good Name. I cannot say much for them myself.

There is then an abrupt change in Sweeney's handwriting from pale, barely distinguishable maroon to ordinary, legible graphite. The letter continues: 'I cannot write with that thing. This bit I have is not as big as my little finger but it is English.'

On the other hand, Private Archie Surfleet, could not praise too highly the generosity of certain French villagers whom he met when out on rest at the time of the Battle of the Somme, being fought some way to the south of their sector, in 1916:

> We called at a house in a little place called Neuf Berquin and asked the people if they would do us a meal, for which, of course, we intended to pay. We were welcomed with open arms and ushered into the best room whilst a beautiful little dinner was got ready for us. When it came to parting, these kindly folks absolutely refused to accept anything at all for it; one does not meet many like that in any country.

47   *Bargaining with the local population; persuasive Tommies in the market place at Bailleul attempting to acquire geese at a favourable price for their Christmas dinner, December 1916. (Q1629)*

Of course, these were ordinary civilians with no commercial interest. Perhaps it was more tempting for those who had the commercial power, however limited, to try in their own way to do well out of the war.

But unfair dealing was not necessarily a monopoly of perfidious Frenchmen: the Tommy could have his perfidious moments too:

> Billeted at Bus-les-Artois, a most respectable village. Some of the inhabitants made a small fortune by providing *'café au lait'* for the troops, but at the same time they probably lost a good many spoons and cups! Unfortunately some of the men looked upon this as desirable plunder, for future use in their billets. This was undoubtedly one of the reasons for the attitude of suspicion shown by the country folk in many places — an attitude which was most strongly condemned by the very men who caused it.
>
> *Private Clifford Carter, Hull Commercials*

The relationship between soldier and civilian was inevitably complicated by the problem of communication. Lance-Corporal Mountfort and his comrades of the 10th Royal Fusiliers — mostly city men from London — might find it relatively easy to maintain an *entente cordiale*

SUZANNE — Café Cavel, Eglise et Mairie

48   *A typical French estaminet, at Suzanne, on the Somme. Quite unlike the public houses of Britain, estaminets had their own special and highly memorable atmosphere. Almost invariably run by a Madame and famous for their weak beer and egg and chips, and other such modest fare, they were the nearest to a soldiers' club for the Tommies of the Western Front. However, Temperance was a powerful cause in Britain at this time, thus many soldiers would never dream of darkening an estaminet's door. (Mr C.E. Owen)*

with the local people, but for most men the French language presented a major problem, if a problem with rich possibilities for comic misunderstanding:

> I expect this is supposed to be a very nice place in peacetime but I think myself it is not half so good as good old England. If you ask the people any question here all they say is 'NO COMPREE', if you want to buy an Egg you have to think of a horse and say *'HOOF'*. Bread is *Du Pain*, butter is *De Burr*, from morning to night it is 'NO COMPREE'.
>
> *Private Jack Sweeney*

> The men's 'French' is most amusing: the usual remark in passing through a town or village is *'Bong joor, madam,* how's your father?' or *'Commont ally voo? Bocoo prommynade!'*
>
> *Second Lieutenant Arthur Gibbs*

Some men, in fact, resorted to sign language, Second Lieutenant Cyril Rawlins, described the resourcefulness of his batman in a letter of June 1915:

My man Bobett nearly makes me die with laughing sometimes as he gesticulates to the peasants for eggs: squatting down, flapping his arms and squawking. He then grunts and makes as if he were slicing bacon. For milk he says 'moo, moo', but you should see him trying to get boot polish.

One thing that always won the admiration of the British troops was the extraordinary resilience of so many French and Belgian civilians and in particular their determination to carry on their normal lives even within range of the guns. Major Walter Vignoles wrote in a letter of February 1916:

There is a house close by where a mother and a daughter are still living. The mother refuses to budge although two shells have burst in the farm, one in the yard outside their living room and one actually in their bedroom. They keep chickens and sell coffee to the soldiers, but appear to have no other means of livelihood.

But the people who won Major Vignoles' supreme accolade were two French ladies who ran a tea-shop in Armentières, even though the town was 'all but deserted, with street after street shut up', and 'notwithstanding that a few shells are sent into the town almost every day':

On each side of it the shops are closed, but in the window of this one was an oil lamp lighting up boxes of chocolate, and a card marked 'Tea Room'. Inside there was a room that would not disgrace London and two charming Mesdemoiselles to serve us. We were late so there was no crowd. We had a chat with the pretty Mlle, who must be known and admired by several thousands of British officers! The house has already been hit by five shells and the upstairs rooms have been wrecked, but there is no sign of this in the tea room. Parker and Anderson of course made eyes at her, and told her we had come quite especially to see her, which she seemed to think quite natural, and one of the two said: 'That is the sort of girl I could easily fall in love with.'

Parker played the piano and it was surprising to see how the men who were there turned round at the tables, to listen more easily. I had noticed before how men appreciate any music, however simple, when they have been in the trenches.

9 'It's unlucky to be killed on a Friday'

'As the soldier approached the front for the first time he was inevitably curious as to how he would stand up to the presence of danger.' This is how Private W.T. Colyer of the Artists' Rifles recorded his reaction to his first shell which exploded at a distance of 30 yards:

> And was I panic-stricken? No. Not in the least. It would be hard to analyse my feelings as I gazed at the ugly brown hole in the green field. Astonishment, excitement, realization, relief, foreboding, curiosity and even a morbid kind of satisfaction — these emotions possessed me almost simultaneously and left no room for the sensation of fear. Nothing to be frightened of in fact — provided it did not burst any closer, that is to say. Ah. that was the question: where was the next one coming?

The real test came when a bombardment was not sporadic but sustained, and when it was virtually impossible to dismiss the thought that the next shell might be considerably nearer than the last. On a September night in 1915 Second Lieutenant Cyril Rawlins led a ration party with six pack-mules up the line through steady shellfire. He described his own and his men's reactions in a letter to his mother:

> The men laugh and joke with each other and speculate on the possibilities of getting a 'blighty' wound. Some of them sing little songs under their breath and try not to think about the bullets: I think we all envy the mules who don't know what it all means. I suppose I must be a bit of a coward myself after all, because I would give anything to be able to run and hurry along, anything but that slow crawling walk: or I would like to get down in a ditch whenever the glaring star shell rises: I want to stoop and hang my head and get down as low as possible. But one must stride along as nonchalantly as if out for a moonlight stroll at home!!! I wonder, do other men have these weird feelings? — things one does not talk about except to one's intimates.

The problem with a man of Rawlins' sensitivity was that he could not avoid the mental speculation as to what might happen when exposed to shot or shell. 'I have too vivid an imagination for a soldier: it's so hard to keep one's mind off the "feel" of bullets entering various parts of one's anatomy.' But his own highly charged and sophisticated reactions led him to comment, perhaps too facilely, on the difference of response, as he saw it, between officers and men — though it is perhaps fair to add that he wrote this in a letter written two months before the journey up the line described in the extract above. 'Our soldiers have no nerves, no imagination, and only one fear, being without a "fag"'.

There is no evidence that fear and imagination were only confined to the well brought up and the highly educated. Indeed a vivid awareness of the possibilities of pain and death could strike any thoughtful soldier whatever his rank. Private Archie Surfleet analysed his feelings in his diary when out on rest after a number of particularly hazardous visits to the line:

> It is easy to sit here in the sunshine all nice and quiet, and write it up now, but there is something akin to great nervous strain to trek there and back, shelled at intervals, losing men killed and wounded on each journey. I don't suppose I shall ever lose my nervousness of shelling and though I may not panic I always have a secret fear at the back of my mind; not maybe, unnatural in a chap raised in peace and security.

There was another element in his anxiety which many others would have understood:

> I keep thinking of the old folks at home. They really are a worry to me. And, windy as I am, I think I am more distressed at the thoughts of their feelings if the worst comes to the worst, than I am afraid for myself.

Equally comprehensible, and no doubt equally widely shared, was the attitude expressed by Private George Morgan, 1st Bradford Pals:

> I was afraid — everyone must have been afraid, but I was more afraid of showing it. I didn't want to let the side down. I hoped I would be able to do what I was expected to do.

Yet there were undoubtedly men who claimed never to be afraid; men who never experienced 'the wind vertical'; men who were able to adopt a totally fatalistic attitude to danger. If a shell or a bullet had your number on it, you would get it; if it didn't you would survive. It was as simple as that:

> I was never frightened. If you were scared you were done for. Thank God I wasn't. I don't know why — I've no idea. As a signaller in the Artillery I often had to go forward with the infantry, paying out my signal wire, but I can't remember ever worrying whether I would be able to do my job or whether I would get to wherever I had to go. And often I had to be on my own, in places where if you had somebody with you it wasn't so bad, but if you had to go forward on your own under heavy shelling you would be bound to think that

if you got knocked out there would be no one to help you. But I was never nervous. How you didn't get blown to atoms you never knew. Your life wasn't yours, it wasn't even yours to think about; it was in the hands of Fate. You were to go or you were not to go; you either got wounded or you didn't. And under no circumstances could you jib or run back: you couldn't. And you couldn't take cover if you were told to go forward. You had to go forward even if you were blown to pieces.

Gunner J.J. Daniells, Royal Field Artillery

Perhaps most remarkable of all was the attitude of such a young officer as Lieutenant Alex Wilkinson, 2nd Battalion Coldstream Guards, when he went into battle on the first day of the Third Battle of Ypres, 31 July 1917:

I felt wonderfully confident about the show. Never for one moment did I have the least anxiety. I knew from the start that I was going through without a touch and in spite of the appalling discomfort I enjoyed it enormously. I would not have missed it for anything. I am only looking forward to the time when we have to do another show.

It might be thought that, among those who took a less fatalistic view, time would make it easier to live with the pressures and dangers around them, that they might even become blasé. Such may have been the case with some men, but with others precisely the opposite was true. When Private Jack Sweeney had his first experience of the front line in November 1914, his reactions were decidedly jaunty — 'there seems to be no Fear in the old Lincolns' — but by October of the next year he was writing in a very different vein: 'I find now that my nerves are all gone and I tremble every time I hear a shell. It is not because I am frightened but I cannot help it at all.' Six months later his mood was equally sombre: his battalion had just gone through a bombardment by trench mortars, a gas attack and a German trench raid: 'I had one of the closest shaves I have ever had but I am safe though badly shaken. I am sure this war will send us all mad, people at home cannot realize what the lads out here have to go through.' In January 1917 he reported

a very bad time in the trenches at Xmas, but the lads that relieved us had it worse, old Fritz took 51 prisoners. I am pleased to tell you that we are resting for a long time, yet I have often wondered how I stick it but I really feel done now and my nerves seem to have all gone but after resting I expect I shall be fit again.

He still had many months of hard fighting ahead, including what he dreaded most of all — a return to 'Worse than Hell', as he called Ypres, during the long-drawn-out battle of 1917 usually known as Passchendaele. On 3 November, just three days before the Passchendaele ridge was captured in almost impossible conditions by the Canadians, he wrote to his fiancée:

I laughed at you dear, getting the wind up when I was home but you should see me shaking like a jelly. Yes this is quite true dear I am not joking. 'Struth it is a rotten war. Fancy lying down under a sheet and the sheet is the only cover to stop the bits of bombs, not very comforting is it dear. Well we all get the wind up and no mistake.

Sweeney was fortunate: a month later a not-too-serious wound but one bad enough to get him back to 'Blighty' put him out of action for the rest of the war; but for men with badly frayed nerves who found no such relief there were worse torments waiting. 'Shell-shock' was a condition to which many men succumbed and which produced, sometimes not only temporarily, a complete disintegration of personality.

It took two years for the military authorities to recognize that 'shell-shock' existed as a definable medical state: the term only became official in 1916. In late 1917 Bombardier Harry Fayerbrother, Royal Field Artillery, found himself with a gun-crew in the Ypres Salient with a seriously shell-shocked comrade.

He upset all of us. There were just five or six of us in our dugout and every time a shell came over he went haywire, shouting and screaming as if he wanted to tear the place to pieces, and tear us to pieces too. We just couldn't put up with it, so I grabbed him by the scruff of the neck and took him down the duckboard track to the dressing station. He was quite a mild little fellow, in fact quite a sweet-natured sort of chap.

It must be readily admitted that this is a very difficult area in which to draw conclusions or attempt generalizations. Men reacted in a wide variety of ways to the extraordinary circumstances in which they found themselves: some could take them in their stride, some could adjust to them with the help of discipline and comradeship, some simply could not cope. Perhaps the best way to conclude this selection of disparate and indeed contradictory experiences is to quote from two soldiers, already much quoted in this book, who wrote, at the time, thoughtfully and with insight about their part in the war.

Lance-Sergeant Elmer Cotton, 5th Battalion Northumberland Fusiliers, made this statement in his notebook of 1915:

The British soldier is a man who knows fear but overcomes it — when in the fight he can be relied upon to see it through but before it begins he is anxious.

Captain Harry Yoxall, 18th Battalion King's Royal Rifles Corps, wrote this in September 1916 during the Battle of the Somme:

Don't believe stories which you see in the papers about troops asking as a special privilege not to be relieved. We stick it, at all costs if necessary, as long as ordered, but everyone's glad to hand over to someone else. And anyone who says he enjoys this kind of thing is either a liar or a madman.

49   *'Smile boys that's the style . . .' British troops in buoyant mood after taking over a former German trench at Serre, on the Somme, in March 1917. (Q1787)*

To a later generation, perhaps over-conditioned by the disenchanted war poetry of writers like Siegfried Sassoon and Wilfred Owen and by the explosion of anti-war literature of the late twenties and thirties, it is a revelation to realize that the Tommy found much to tease his humour in the life of the Western Front. Sassoon might write of the 'hell where youth and laughter go'; but in that hell laughter, if somewhat grimly, managed to survive. As Private A.L. Atkins, 17th Battalion Middlesex Regiment, commented in a post-war memoir: 'Even in the most dire circumstances, shell-fire, machine-gun fire, knee-deep in mud and water, with short rations and pay-day just a distant memory (4/8d a week in my case), most of us still found time for a laugh and a joke.'

Second Lieutenant Cyril Rawlins spent some time as battalion censor; he found the reading of his soldiers' letters to be more than merely a tedious chore:

> One gets a good insight into the inner working of the Tommy's mind in this way: there never was a more cheerful, philosophical, kindly creature than the British soldier; his humour is inimitable and equal to any emergency.

The humour is not public house or music hall: it provokes the wry smile rather than the belly laugh: it comes right out of the situations in which the men found themselves. Major Vignoles, Grimsby Chums, collected one or two of the spontaneous witticisms of his men and recorded them in his letters home:

50 *Few things cheered the Tommy's heart more than the acquisition of souvenirs, and few items were higher in the list of favoured trophies than the German 'pickelhaube'. This photograph, also showing a proudly displayed enemy shell-case, was taken in late 1916 at the end of the Battle of the Somme. (Mr John Robson)*

Our ration party was paddling along in the water one day, carrying their bags on their shoulders, all were quiet being very tired, when some wag at the front says: 'Pass it on, KEEP A SHARP LOOK OUT FOR SUBMARINES', and so the message was passed on by every man, perfectly solemnly without laughing at all! The Tommies are very quaint sometimes.

Sloshing through mud and water seems to have produced a rich vein of comment at all times. Sergeant Robert McKay, 109th Field Ambulance, 36th (Ulster) Division, was on his way to the front just before the opening of the Battle of the Somme when he and his comrades came to

a very deep shell-hole. I waded in until the water was up to my armpits and was just getting out on the other side when I heard a loud laugh and splashing behind me. I looked back and could just see a tin hat moving across the surface of the water. One of the others called out. 'This is our first casualty, not shot but drowned!' Gradually, however, a head, and then the remainder of the body emerged from the muddy water and I realized it was Joe Allen. Joe was only about 5 feet 2 inches in height and he had sunk into the deepest part of the shell hole.

51, 52 *A typical concert programme, with numerous local jokes. A Second Lieutenant wrote of such concerts: 'Everybody is ready to laugh at everything and mirth is the predominant feature of the whole performance.' (Mr F.W. Doyle)*

¶ Discussions on LEAVE are prohibited, as the Artistes are "Full of Hope."

★ ★

¶ The Shell-hole adjoining the Theatre is the property of the Company and must not be taken away.

★ ★

¶ Any member of the audience showing one or more green envelopes does so at his own risk.

★ ★

¶ ALL Ranks are notified that our Leading Lady is "Out of Bounds."

★ ★

¶ Patrons are requested to note that they can pay without coming in, but cannot come in without paying.

★ ★

¶ During the remainder of the War no person will be admitted to this theatre in Evening Dress.

★ ★

¶ Patrons are requested to refrain from falling off the balconies.

★ ★

¶ Our Shrapnel is the best, refuse all imitations.

★ ★

¶ Working parties supplied with (*very*) light refreshments.

The 55th Divisional Theatre Coy.

PRESENT

Their Third Revue

ENTITLED

"THUMBS"

IN THREE SCENES

WRITTEN AND PRODUCED BY THE COMPANY

Wigs by W. CLARKSON
Costumes by W. CLARKSON and MORRIS ANGEL.

FOR THE DIVISIONAL THEATRE :

Stage Manager and Carpenter - Sapper A. HORRIDGE
Electricians - - - J. HURLEY & Pte. ROBOTHAM
Engineer - - - - - Pte. C. HALL
Cinema Operators - { Trooper REYNOLDS
                      Ptes. BUDD & RAMSDEN
Scenic Artist - - - - Lce.-Cpl. G. PAGE

Orchestra under the Direction of Pte. COUPE, consisting of
A. HONDERWOOD, R. ROBINSON & J. FULLERTON

Prices of Admission :

Officers—Box Seats - - - - - - 2 Frs.
Balcony - - - - - - 1 „
Sergeants - - - - - - - 50 Cts.
Other Ranks - - - - - - 30 „

This Programme is subject to alteration

53, 54   *The First Army
Concert Party* Les
Rouges et les Noirs,
*also known, English
style, as* The Reds and
the Blacks. *The ladies
in the general photograph
above, and 'Gwen',
right, are, of course,
soldiers in drag: hence the
statement in the
programme opposite:
'ALL Ranks are notified
that our Leading Lady is
"Out of Bounds".'*
(Mrs M. Leeke)

At times, however, the context could be positively macabre. The following are memories of autumn 1916, during the Somme battle.

> Along the road was an unburied hand of a soldier, some of our 'wags' would pretend to shake hands with it — a bit of humour along the way.
> *Lieutenant Fred R. Wells, 47th Bn Canadian Expeditionary Force*

> On the day we took Thiepval — it was one of the greatest days in our Battalion's history — our movement to the forming up line was by a communication trench called Pip Street. At one point a dead soldier's lower leg was protruding from the side of the trench. It was covered, to some extent, by what had obviously been a green silk sock; the good quality of the article was still obvious. With a loud 'Lor' Bill! What a toff!' one of our men, a worthy from Stratford E., passed on to his battle position.
> *Captain R.A. Chell, 10th Bn Essex Regt*

By contrast the Tommy was not above a bit of innocent fun to amuse the local people:

> We marched back to Béthune and some of our men afforded amusement to the inhabitants by wearing German helmets with sausages stuck on the spikes which they found in the captured German dugouts.
> *Rifleman A.H. Young, 1/15th Bn London Regt, London Irish Rifles*

One young officer who not only tuned in instantly with soldierly humour but also led and enriched it was the artist and wit Bruce Bairnsfather, who went to France in 1914 as a subaltern of the Royal Warwickshire Regiment. Creator of the archetypal curmudgeonly but dogged Tommy figure 'Ole Bill', he brilliantly caught the prevailing mood in a series of near-subversive cartoons. These were too much for the authorities at first and he was subject to official censure, but later they conceded and from 1916 he was attached to the War Office as an officer cartoonist. His most famous effort showed two soldiers in a shell hole under heavy bombardment with a caption which became one of the legendary 'sayings' of the war: 'Well, if you knows of a better 'ole, go to it.' Originally appearing in the London-based magazine *The Bystander*, the cartoon became an icon of its time, its tag-line being quoted on an infinity of occasions, never more movingly than on the tragic first day on the Somme, when the CO of the 1st Hampshires, the Hon. L.C.W. Palk, lying mortally wounded in a shell hole in No Man's Land, turned to a man lying near him and said, 'If you know of a better 'ole, go to it'. Recording the event in his *Personal Record of the War*, his friend Brigadier-General H.C. Rees commented: 'That kind of spirit does great things and it is lucky for the Germans that they were able to prevent us getting on even terms with them.'

Humour was indeed about spirit and morale, but it was also about mockery, about finding a safety valve for the release of tension and frustration. Most connoisseurs of First World War literature are familiar with that remarkable production *The Wipers Times*, sustained over two-and-three-quarter years with various changes of title (for example, *The*

Somme Times, The BEF Times and finally, *The Better Times,* for its edition of December 1918). It blithely cocked the snook at military bluster and pomposity and even teased generals and the military establishment, while never questioning the basic ethos of the campaign. But it was founded by officers and its humour was largely officerial in character. The following items, the origins of which are almost certainly lost in the folklore of the front, have an earthier 'other ranks' ring. Here surely is the droll, tongue-in-cheek attitude of the Poor Bloody Infantryman, authentically preserved:

STANDING ORDERS FOR BRITISH INFANTRY IN FRANCE

1. The Colonel is thine only Boss; thou shalt have no other Boss but him.

2. But thou shalt make unto thyself many graven images of officers who fly in the heavens above, Staff Officers who own the Earth beneath, and of Submarine Officers who are in the waters under the earth. Thou shalt stand up and salute them for the Colonel thy boss will visit with Field Punishment unto the 1st & 2nd degree on those that salute not, and shower stripes on them that salute and obey his commandments.

3. Thou shalt not take the name of the Adjutant in vain for the Colonel will not hold him guiltless who taketh the Adjutant's name in vain.

4. Remember thou shalt not rest on the Sabbath day. Six days shalt thou labour and not do all thy work but the 7th day is the day of the CRE [Commander Royal Engineers]; on it thou shalt do all manner of work & thy officers & thy NCO's & thy sanitary men & the Kitchener's Army who are within thy trench for instruction.

5. Honour the Army Staff that thy days may be long in the Corps Reserve where one day they may send thee.

6. Thou shalt kill only Huns, slugs, lice, rats & other vermin which frequent dug-outs.

7. Thou shalt not adulterate thy Section's rum ration.

8. Thou shalt not steal or at any rate not be found out.

9. Thou shalt not bear false witness in the orderly room.

10. Thou shalt not covet the ASC's job, nor his pay, nor his motors, nor his wagons, nor his tents, nor his billets, nor his horses, nor his asses, nor any cushy thing that is his.

(It should be commented that the ASC — the Army Service Corps — was the object of much envy on the part of the men in the firing line. Their pay could be as much as six times as high as that of an ordinary infantryman and they were usually well clear of shells and bullets. Ironically, the pay of those most exposed was the lowest of all.)

Also in the same cynically humorous vein are these 'Soldiers Superstitions':

It is unlucky for 13 to sit down to a meal when rations have been issued for only 7.
If the sun rises in the East, it is a sure sign that there will be stew for dinner.
To drop your rifle on foot of a second lieutenant is bad luck — for him. To drop ditto on foot of sergeant major is bad luck — for you.

To hear lecture on glorious history of your Regiment indicates that you will shortly be going 'over the top'.

If a new officer, on taking over trench, announces that he has learned all about it at Cadet School, sign that he is about to get a surprise.

Perhaps a special place of honour should be reserved for the superstition which normally appears at the head of the list quoted above:

It is considered very unlucky to be killed on a Friday.

1   *Eric Kennington,*
     'A Famous
     Raider of the
     Lancashire
     Fusiliers':
     lithograph

2   *Eric Kennington,*
     'Back to Billets':
     pastel

3 C.R.W. Nevinson, 'A Group of Soldiers': oil on canvas, 1917. This picture drew criticism from the censor of images, Colonel A.N. Lee, who thought that the type of man represented in it was unworthy of the British Army, to which the artist replied, 'if you would just let me know what you consider a pretty man, I will in future paint all my soldiers up to your ideal, only I must know what it is.'

4 Gilbert Rogers, 'Mud': oil on canvas

5   *Augustus John, 'Fraternity': oil on canvas. Virtually a straight copy of a well-known mass-circulation postcard 'A Fag after a Fight',* Daily Mail Official War Pictures, *Series 2, No. 11*

6   *'Back to Blighty (study from life)'; a much reproduced tinted photogravure by the well-known photographer F.J. Mortimer, showing a mud-spattered private of a Territorial infantry regiment, circa late 1915. He is wearing a peaked cap with earflaps (known as the 'Gorblimey') under a rubberised cotton cap cover, a greatcoat, a sheepskin jacket, and is carrying various packs including an early anti-phosgene helmet gas-mask satchel*

Killing Germans

7   *E. Handley-Read, 'Killing Germans: the machine at work': charcoal and water-colour*

8   *Majory Watherston, 'The Dispatch (The Captain's Dugout)': oil on canvas, 1917*

9   *James Prinsep Beadle, 'Zero Hour': oil on canvas*

Blowing bodies to smithereens.

10 (Above) Gunner
Hiram sturdy:
'Blowing bodies to
smithereens': pen and
water-colour

11 Revd Canon Cyril
Lomax, 'Last time over
the bags was terrible ...'
Lomax served in
France between July
1916 and April 1917
as chaplain to the 8th
Battalion Durham
Light Infantry; the
drawing and 'caption'
are part of one of his
letters, almost certainly
written during the later
stages of the Somme
battle, though its precise
date is unfortunately not
known.
Pen and water-colour

Last time over the bags was rather terrible. The few
who managed to pull themselves out of the waist deep mud
had to stand on the top & pull others who were stuck out of the
trenches. Imagine doing that with machine guns hard at
work to say nothing of snipers. One man I know of was
drowned in the mud. Another was only extricated by eight
men. Naturally no supports or rations could come up, &
after gaining their objective in some cases, in others being
mown down at once they had to retire.
I have had to make this trench too wide

12   *Gunner Hiram Sturdy: 'Wire uncut. He bows, "My show is over boys". Your call now.': pen and water-colour*

ARRAS   CAMBRIA   ROAD
APRIL   1914.

Wire uncut. He bows, "My show is over boys" You're call now.

The shell-holes are full of bodies

13   *Gunner Hiram Sturdy: 'The shell-holes are full of bodies': pen and water-colour*

14   *C.R.W. Nevinson, 'Tank': oil on canvas*

15   *John Singer Sargent, 'Camouflaged Tanks, Berles-au-Bois': water-colour, 1918*

16   Haydn Reynolds Mackey, 'Epéhy, 1918': oil on canvas

17   Henry Tonks, 'An Advanced Dressing Station in France, 1918': oil on canvas

18   Four paintings by J. Hodgson Lobley, all oil on canvas: 'Loading Wounded at Boulogne'

19   'Charing Cross Station: Detraining wounded by the British Red Cross and the Order of St.
      John', 1919

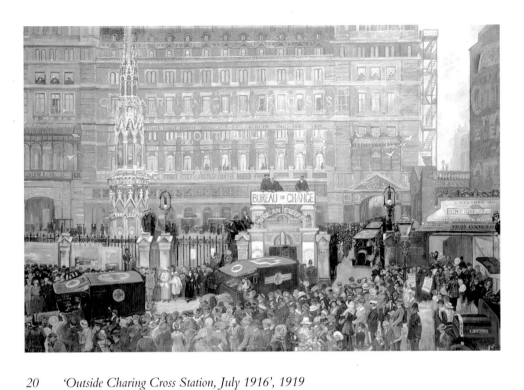

20   'Outside Charing Cross Station, July 1916', 1919

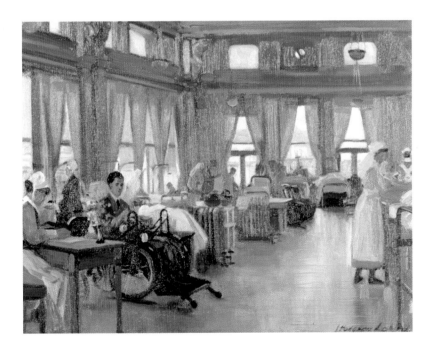

21   'The Special Surgical Auxiliary Hospital at the "Star and Garter" Richmond: the dining room', 1919

22   E. Handley-Read, 'Bernafay Wood, Looking towards Trônes Wood', Somme battlefield: charcoal and wash

23   John Nash, 'Oppy Wood, 1917, Evening': oil on canvas

24   *John Louis Ginnett, 'Ypres Salient, Dawn, February 1918': oil on canvas*

25   *Paul Nash, 'The Ypres Salient at Night': oil on canvas, 1918*

26   Fortunino Matania, 'The Last Message': oil on canvas

27   C.R.W. Nevinson, 'Paths of Glory': oil on canvas, 1917. Although this now celebrated
      painting was judged unsuitable for exhibition at his second one-man show at the Leicester
      galleries, London, in March 1918, Nevinson nevertheless displayed it, with a sheet of brown
      paper across it reading CENSORED

28   *C.R.W. Nevinson, 'The Harvest of Battle': oil on canvas, 1919*

Colour illustrations

29   Wartime: men of an East Yorkshire Regiment picking their way around shell craters,
Frezenberg, Ypres Salient, September 1917. One of the classic silhouette photographs by
official photographer Ernest Brooks. Tinted

30   Postwar: the 41st Division Memorial at Flers, Somme battlefield.

10 'Just a line to say I go "over the top" tomorrow'

However much he might become accustomed to the routines of trench warfare, the Tommy knew that in time he would almost certainly have to face a still greater ordeal. Sooner or later the moment would arrive when he would have to leave the relative security of his trenches and advance towards the enemy in open battle.

The intention behind the British doctrine of maintaining the offensive spirit even in the quieter times and the cushier trenches — and behind the acceptance of trenches recognizably inferior in quality to those on the other side of the wire — was to instil in the soldiers the firm understanding that he was only there for the time being: until his leaders could mount the massive assault which would put the enemy to flight and drive him back towards Berlin. Trench routine, in fact, was merely a holding operation: the essential act of war was the set-piece attack: in the parlance of the time, 'the Big Push'.

Major Walter Vignoles of the Grimsby Chums put the point in young officers' language before the 'Push' of 1916 in the event that was to become known to history as the Battle of the Somme. As the massive preliminary bombardment continued day after day, he wrote: 'When one thinks about it all, or stops to analyse it, it seems an extraordinary "game" — the awful waste — but the only thing to do is to go on and try to "biff the Boche".' It was, indeed, the only thing to do, so long as the Western Front remained, as it did remain, the principal theatre of the war. It was here that, to borrow Churchill's phrase, the 'World Crisis' was to be resolved. And it was to be resolved by the energy, the fighting capacity, and, as everyone knew, the sacrifice of thousands and thousands of men.

For the infantryman this was the ultimate experience: it was for this he had joined up. He had not volunteered to hold alien ground indefinitely in a muddy warren of rat-infested trenches, but to right the wrongs of France, avenge little Belgium, and, in C.E. Montague's phrase, 'reclaim the world for straightness and decency'. To achieve these ends he had to attack the enemy and beat him; and to do that he would have to go 'over the top'.

'Over the top', 'over the lid', 'over the bags' (i.e. the sandbags that formed the trench wall) — there were a number of versions of this 'fateful phrase', as one infantryman called it, but whatever expression he used it expressed a daunting concept for the soldier. The prospects of being killed or mutilated were high. If a man was wounded in a trench stretcher-bearers were usually on hand to take him quickly down to the dressing station. If he was wounded among the shell holes and barbed wire entanglements of No Man's Land, he might bleed slowly and painfully to death with no one to help him or relieve his

55   *Fixing scaling ladders in trenches on 8 April 1917, the day before the opening of the Battle of Arras. (Q6229)*

sufferings. But these possibilities had to be faced if the goal for which everyone had trained and striven over the weeks and months of preparation were to be achieved.

The letters and diaries of the time show no unanimity of reaction among the soldiers about to go into battle. Predictably men faced the prospect of action in a wide variety of ways: some with jaunty confidence, many more with a thoughtful and reconciled awareness, others with unashamed loathing and apprehension.

The extracts that follow all date from the last days before the opening of the Battle of the Somme on 1 July 1916. This was a particularly significant and emotional time for the volunteer soldiers of Britain. It was to be the first blooding of the men of Kitchener's Army. The Pals Battalions were there in strength. Confidence was, on the whole, remarkably high. The preparations, it seemed, had been as thorough as they could be. Throughout the last weeks of June — during which period most of the letters that follow were written — a bombardment of colossal intensity, reputedly the greatest the world had ever seen, pulverized the enemy trenches. The optimistic forecasts of the commanders predicted a virtual walk-over. (Indeed, the tactics chosen by the General in charge of the opening phase of the battle, Sir Henry Rawlinson, dictated that the attacking troops were literally to walk across No Man's Land, heavily laden with equipment, at 7.30 on a summer's morning.) Everyone knew, however, that the German was a formidable opponent. Even if the first wave were to stroll to its objectives — which in the event it did not — there would be bound to be fierce resistance sooner or later and, inevitably, many casualties.

This letter was written by Lieutenant Robert Sutcliffe. At 38 he was older than most of his comrades: a successful Bradford solicitor, a well-known amateur golfer and a distinguished old boy of Bradford Grammar School. He had joined up as a member of the Public Schools' Battalion and later been commissioned in the 1st Bradford Pals:

> Just a line to say I go 'over the lid' tomorrow. My company are in the first line of attack and hope to do great things. We all naturally hope to come through all right, but, of course, one never knows, someone's bound to go under and it's the only way to end the war. It's a great thing to be in, and I'm glad our division is one of the first chosen to go over.

Sutcliffe's 31st Division, entirely consisting of 'pals' battalions, would suffer heavily on 1 July and his battalion would suffer over 500 casualties. Twenty-two of its officers would be killed or wounded. Sutcliffe himself died at sea while being evacuated by hospital ship to England. He is buried not with his 'Pals' of the 16th Battalion of the West Yorkshire Regiment in the cemeteries on the Serre road in Picardy, but in a quiet graveyard in the Pennine Hills a dozen miles from Bradford.

This letter was written by Lieutenant William Clarke, Sheffield City Battalion, also in 31st Division, to his fiancée, on 29 June:

> My Own Sweetheart,
> I have just been busy sending off letters to various people and before lying down must send my wee girl a few lines.
> I got your letter today and you seem quite cheery so as long as Dora's all right 'All's well with the world'.
> Now my sweetheart I am going off to get some sleep. All my love darling girl and keep a brave heart for my sake and just pray that this war will soon be over and I can come back to take care of you and never leave you anymore.
> All my love and lots of sweet kisses.
> Willie

Lieutenant Clarke was killed in action on 1 July. His battalion too, having attacked almost 800 strong, suffered over 500 casualties.

This letter was written by a Kitchener volunteer of 49 to his 14-year-old son:

> To my Own Dear Boy Jimmy,
> . . . I am well content knowing my loved ones at Home are thinking of their Dad and doing the best they can to brighten one another's lives. Your sweet Mother tells me that you do try and be a Comfort to her and it takes the weariness off my shoulders over this War and I can fight with a better heart

56   *One of the mass of guns firing during the week-long bombardment which preceded the Battle of the Somme. Major Walter Vignoles wrote: 'The noise is terrific . . . it is a series or succession of huge bangs, developing at times into a continuous roar . . . The whole air throbs with the sound . . . it seems to come in huge sudden stabs.' (Q46)*

when everything is going on all right at Home. So now my Dearest Boy look
Upward and Go Forward in the Right is the Earnest Wish of
Your Affectionate
Father.

The writer was reported missing in the battle and later presumed dead: he became one of
the 73,000 dead of the Somme whose bodies were never found.[1]

The following extracts are from a letter written by Private Arthur Hubbard, London
Scottish, to his two sisters. The letter was begun on 29 June:

Hope we shall be successful on Saturday morning July 1st at dawn when you
are all fast asleep in driving the Huns out of their present position, and without
any bad luck to myself. I have got to go over with the first batch, and assist in
cutting the barb wire [sic] which hasn't been destroyed by our artillery during
the past few days heavy bombardment . . . I should be in my glory if the news
came through to cease firing and pack up . . . I can imagine how everything
looks at home, and the garden as you say must be almost at its best, you will

57   *German trenches under artillery barrage prior to the Somme attack. Lieutenant Kenneth Macardle wrote: 'All along the Bosch front line black and yellow, white and grey puffs of smoke dance in mighty cruel glee; fountains of brown sand or black clay shoot up high carrying with them a bunch of stakes all tangled up with wire . . . The heavy shells throw back volumes of smoke some 300 feet into the air.' (Q23)*

soon be having beans I presume. I shall imagine I am in heaven when I get home, what a treat it will be to feel nice and clean, at present it is up to your neck in mud, which all helps to make you feel miserable. I am sorry to have to state all this, but I don't feel inclined to tell you a pack of lies, if the truth were told a bit more often, I don't suppose the war would be on now, when you land over here they have got you tight and treat you as they think.

Friday June 30th. We are just going to have an open air Church service, and are going to the trenches this evening, ready for the attack in the morning, so I think this is all I have to say until this affair is over, hoping to write a longer letter to Heather and you all on Sunday if I get through alright, which I very much hope I shall successfully, so must close with my best love to you all at home.

I Remain,

Your Affec Brother

Arthur

Private, later Corporal, Hubbard survived the attack and the war but, as will be described in Chapter 11, was never to recover from his experiences on the Somme. His letter also includes an account of an episode by no means unique before a great battle: 'I was 20 yds from one of the Kensington's 13th London Regt, last week, when he shot himself through the foot just to get back to England out of it, of course he will get about 84 days field punishment for it, after the wound has healed up. I went over and fetched assistance to him and extracted the empty case out of his rifle, what a feeling he will have later on if it takes a long time to heal up and to know he (has) done it himself, but still he is not the only one that has done likewise.'

Second Lieutenant Kenneth Macardle, 17th Battalion Manchester Regiment, wrote the following in his diary shortly before the battle opened. He was the archetypal young officer who found great exhilaration in war; he was already famous in his battalion for his expertise and coolness in No Man's Land (see Chapter 7). His diary reflects the high optimism that was the prevalent doctrine of the time; there is no hint of personal doubts or uncertainty:

> Rumour says we are to smash the Hun line altogether, shove in our army de chasse and finish the war . . . Rumour also says that we have given Germany four days to declare peace or take the consequences. I am not addicted to boasting but I think if he could see all the guns behind, all the grenades, trench mortars and other stores in front, if he knew how thoroughly ready we are, and if he could conceive how we are longing for 'the day' — I think if he knew, the Kaiser would cut his losses and — take poison.

Second Lieutenant Macardle would be killed just a few days later in the opening stages of the Somme battle.

There could be few more moving accounts of the thoughts and experiences of a young and highly sensitive man about to face the ordeal of battle than that left by Second Lieutenant Roland Ingle of the 9th Lincolns. His all-too-brief diary begins at 5.30 p.m. on Saturday 24 June 1916 and ends at 7 p.m. on Friday 30 June, just $12\frac{1}{2}$ hours before the first-wave attack:

> *Saturday, June 24th*
> The bombardment for the 'great push' has just begun: I am sitting out here on an old plough in a half-tilled field watching the smoke of the shells rising over the German lines. In the hollow straight in front lies the town with its broken church, with the long straight road leading to the rear: there is the village that I was in last Saturday in a hollow to the right, with its small church spire intact showing among the trees. It is a pleasant rather cloudy day, after a night of heavy rain: and the light breeze blowing from the west lessens for us the sound of the guns, besides being a protection, as far as we know, against gas . . . On the whole the evening is 'a pleasant one for a stroll' with the larks singing.

58   *'I went to Communion this morning and knelt in the long grass beneath the blue sky': Lance-Corporal Roland Mountfort shortly before going into action on the Somme. The photograph shows a church parade of the 17th Battalion Liverpool Regiment at Carnoy Valley on 29 June 1916. (Q4069)*

Sunday June 25th

I went up the hill again last night after mess — about 10 o'clock . . . It was of course a wonderful sight: flashes right and left caught your eye in quick succession, and all the time beyond was the red burst of the shells falling on their target. I stood some time looking and two sergeants came up — we talked the usual gossip that we had all heard: any story passes these days and the funny thing is that no one seems to mind if it is something in our favour or decidedly against us. I have heard two distinct rumours that the anxious would find unpalatable: one, that a doctor went over to the Germans from the division on our right, of course, with plenty of valuable information: another that our latest and most wonderful aeroplane settled peacefully behind the Huns' lines. Nobody worries if they are true or not. As the time for us to move approaches I suppose we shall be excited and nervous, but now for most people, and I should think for the most thoughtless and unimpressionable, it is just a contemplative pause and a rest. Excitement braces the muscles in healthy people, and that is the feeling you have at the thought of the 'great push' beginning. As an alternative to trench warfare it is welcome — to me especially, with my doubtful powers of endurance.

59　*Briefing before battle: men of the 1st Battalion Lancashire Fusiliers being addressed by their Divisional Commander, General Sir Beauvoir de Lisle, 29 June 1916. (Q738)*

Someone made the inevitable remark in the mess the other night that we are taking part in what may be a historic event for us, personally, of course, historic but also possibly in years to come a historic event of the Great War. One man's part in any move nowadays is so small that he is not likely to be nervous about the effect of his work on the final result: and fortunately the habit of 'carrying on' (that immortal phrase) is by this time so ingrained in him that in spite of great shattering of everything else [sic] he has a hope that he will be able to do it. And no one should forget that a free throwing of yourself into a forward move gives the thing a momentum that nothing else can — beyond any mechanical discipline. If the least thoughtful could analyse his feelings, he would say, I suppose, that provided he was hitting hard he didn't care what happened to him. And the men who are going to be knocked out in the push — there must be many — should not certainly be looked on with pity: because going forward with resolution and braced muscles puts a man in a mood to despise consequences: he is out to give more than he gets: he really dies fighting, and a man who is used to sport, takes things — even in the great chance of life and death — as part of the game.

This is a remarkable statement and is perhaps worthy of comment. To a later generation — groomed to a diametrically opposite view of war by precisely the kind of event in which Ingle was about to be engaged — to write of a major battle as though it were a somewhat more than usually vigorous soccer or rugby match might seem quaint and naïve. It would, I believe, be uncharitable to think it so. Roland Ingle was a product of the British public school system and of Oxbridge: an old boy of King's School, Ely, a former open scholar at Cambridge, and in the last years before the war a Worcestershire schoolmaster. Like so many of his kind he was a keen sportsman, a cricketer ('a splendid field, especially at point', according to his family) and a good soccer player (he missed his Cambridge Blue through injury). But at 28, and known as a highly intelligent and sensitive young man, he was no doughty jingo eager to kill Germans and have a crack at the Hun. He had joined up because it had seemed his patriotic duty to do so. To go into battle was a necessary corollary of that decision. And for a man brought up in this particular tradition, with no thought of becoming a soldier until the sudden crisis of 1914, what other comparisons were there than the field of sport, with its tensions, its pre-match nerves, its requirement to perform stylishly and to effect and its obligation to attempt to achieve victory? It was, indeed, almost automatic at the time to compare war to a game. 'It seems an extraordinary game,' Major Vignoles wrote, less than half a mile away from Ingle, in the same week. Several miles to the south east Captain Wilfred Nevill, at about the same time, presented two footballs to the leading companies of the 8th East Surreys, which they would kick 'over the top' at zero hour: a ruse that would be presented as heroic by the British press and mocked as 'an English absurdity' by the German; Nevill's own death as he strolled smoking a cigarette towards the enemy lines in the first moments of the attack would only add to this episode's curious renown. Elsewhere a battalion would advance to the attack on 1 July to the sound of a hunting horn. The long months of attrition ahead would put paid to such sporting gestures, but it is entirely comprehensible that they should have been made at this time — before the new, highly dangerous game fully established its own brutal rules of play.

Having resolved his philosophical attitude, Second Lieutenant Ingle then proceeds, reasonably calmly, with the preparations for the battle. There is only one further reference to the prospect of action. 'Everyone is pleased with the idea of going forward: it should relieve the pressure on Verdun, which has been applied purely with the object of delaying and embarrassing our offensive.' For the most part he is content to chronicle the pattern of the days' events — bouts of last-minute training, company 'pow-wows', superintending the moving of ammunition up to the forward emplacements (he was an officer in a Trench Mortar Battery). There are moments of half-amused irony:

> I went up the hill again last night, with three or four others and a gramophone; we took up a position and watched the bombardment, which was still lively and had increased to a continuous roar by the time we came down at 11: the gramophone discoursing 'Comfort ye, comfort ye, my people'! was a curious accompaniment to the guns.

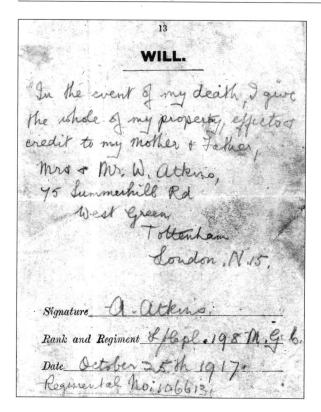

13

WILL.

'In the event of my death, I give the whole of my property, effects & credit to my mother & father, Mrs & Mr. W. Atkins, 75 Summerhill Rd West Green, Tottenham London, N.15,

Signature *A. Atkins.*

Rank and Regiment *L/Cpl. 198 M.G.C.*

Date *October 25th 1917.*

Regimental No: 106613.'

60 *A soldier's will, written in his pay-book. Another form of pre-battle preparation wisely encouraged by the Army. This soldier survived. (IWM Department of Documents)*

He describes a nearby military cemetery:

> The cemetery lies on the right of the road going up to the château; whenever you go by, there is some mound of new earth thrown up. The graves are beautifully kept, and the crosses made in various patterns all carefully done by the pioneer battalion who are responsible for these things. Often you see figures or inscriptions carved in chalk placed on the graves, or, on the cross itself the dead man's cap. Often there are flowers, and men — pals from the dead man's company — tending the graves. The cemetery is in a quiet open space in the middle of the wood, just by the road: on one side were the cookers — the field kitchens — on the other concealed guns, firing their perpetual salute over the graves.

He visits the battalion 'canteen village', as he calls it:

> I got to the village in time to draw 125 francs from the field cashier and then I went to tea at the officers' tea-shop where was a great squash: I read a paper, *The Daily Chronicle* of Wednesday, while waiting for tea and after tea bought milk and fruit and bread, butter and coffee for our mess. Madame stowed the tins in my haversack on my back and I carried some in a side-haversack and I came away.

Later the same day he records

> 'a fat meal' as the result of my shopping — tinned chicken, very little and very expensive at 3 francs: tinned apricots and condensed milk.

He also notes, in the same entry, the death of a friend:

> Today one of C Company officers of the Lincolns (the Company I was in) was killed: Rowe his name was. He acted as second in command of the company during the move from Gandspette. I liked him, he was good-natured and straightforward.

His last entry, which he signed at the end so that it could be sent home as a letter, is written quite coolly and without any demonstration of emotion. The tone, if it can be interpreted at all, is one of quiet acceptance:

> We are moving up to the château tonight and having breakfast there at 3.30. We moved 200 rounds from dugouts to our gun emplacements this afternoon, which took from 3.0–5.30. Our guns were firing all the time and the Huns making some return.
>
> It was a lovely afternoon with a fresh wind blowing: some of the trenches were badly knocked about. I looked over into Hunsland as I came out — the wood in front looking like currant bushes with the blight.
>
> Some trees were down in our wood. I passed the cemetery as I came back and looked at Rowe's grave. I am moving up by myself at 8.30, having a little time here to wash and have a meal. I had three letters to night and *The Observer*, rather delayed, all posted on Sunday.
>
> This ends the diary before the push as I must pack up.
>> Ever yours,
>> Ro

Second Lieutenant Roland Ingle was killed on the morning of 1 July. He is buried in the cemetery which he had described with such careful detail just a few days previously.

---

[1] This simply expressed but profoundly moving letter, faithfully preserved for 60 years, was lent to me by the writer's son, Mr James Hargreaves. Mr Hargreaves wrote: 'I am proud to show you the calibre of these men who gave their lives for their country on that fateful day in 1916.'

11 Into Battle: 'A Great Thing to be in'

Just before dusk on 30 June 1916, a young Lieutenant of the Royal Field Artillery, Cyril Drummond, rode towards the British trenches opposite Thiepval to reconnoitre the route by which his battery was due to advance if the attack went well the following morning. His purpose was to see where and for how long the battery would present a target to the enemy's artillery. It was a relatively quiet and peaceful evening: the British guns were firing but there was no response from the Germans and everything seemed relaxed and outwardly calm. Somewhere in the dead ground behind the trench lines he received a harsh reminder of the reality of war:

> Lying beside a pile of boxes was the body of a soldier who had been killed earlier in the day. He was covered by a blanket, but one corner was awry, exposing an arm, torn, shattered, and dusty. Suddenly, for the first time, the thought crossed my mind, 'Shall I be looking like that this time tomorrow?'

Everywhere about him along the 18-mile front — to the north as far as Gommecourt, to the south-east as far as Montauban — many thousands of men were preparing themselves for battle, some in the trenches, some on the march, some waiting in their billet villages for the order to move forward. Apprehensions of the kind experienced by Lieutenant Drummond must have afflicted many at this time.

At Bus-les-Artois, the 93rd Infantry Brigade, of 31st Division, gathered on the village green and listened to a concert by the Band of the Leeds Pals. Sixty years later a Bradford Pal recalled the mood of the occasion:

> Although I cannot remember the programme played on that lovely summer evening so long ago, I certainly have an abiding memory of one piece — Schubert's *Unfinished Symphony*. Because of this, every performance that I have heard of it since takes me back to that evening in Bus, still quite clear in my mind's eye, with all those Leeds and Bradford Pals sitting around on the grass, quietly listening, and with all of them no doubt wondering, as I certainly did, what awaited us at daybreak the following morning.
>
> *Private W. Slater, 2nd Bradford Pals*

Elsewhere men were marching. A stretcher-bearer in the 19th Division, watching the divisional infantry march off from Laviéville towards the trenches near Albert, was much taken by the fact that

> men of the Welsh Regiments sang most of the time: sang quite softly and — strangely enough — hymns. Accompanied by the muffled shuffling of many feet, this singing in the darkness intensified the eerie unreality of it all.
>
> *Private A. L. Linfoot, 5th Field Ambulance, 57th Brigade*

But a battalion of Northumberland Fusiliers heard a very different sound that evening; a raucous anonymous voice which hailed them as they marched towards the front line:

> You came of your own accord,
> You didn't have to be fetched:
> You *bloody* fools! [1]

Generally, however, this was a time when, whatever private apprehensions men might feel, the mood of the majority of soldiers was one of optimism, and morale and hopes were high. The previous night, 29 June, Major Vignoles, Grimsby Chums, had parted from the officers of his company who were not to go over in the attack:

> They shook hands with us all when they left, and went off not at all pleased at being out of the show. We, on the other hand, were in very good spirits: I don't know why, for we all knew that there was a good chance of many being killed or wounded, but we WERE in good spirits and they were not assumed either — even those who grouse as a rule were cheerful. I think the fact that at last we hoped to get to close quarters with the Boche and defeat him accounted for it.

Private Linfoot, watching his comrades of 19th Division assemble on the last night before the battle, sensed a similar buoyant mood:

> They were massing to go 'over the top' — fateful words for all infantrymen. They were intensely excited yet quietly confident. This was to be the big breakthrough to end the stalemate; to end the war. The timid were less fearful, the bold more exultant, and were thrilled and intensely alive as they 'fell in' on the evening of 30 June. In Laviéville a troop of cavalry trotted past them two by two. Sombre enough in their drab khaki, but in the eyes of their trench-dwelling comrades romantic and splendid. A good omen, surely!

The cavalry, in fact, were to play virtually no part in the ensuing battle; the infantry were to be cut down in their thousands. On the following day, 1 July 1916, there would be (according to the official statistics) 57,470 British casualties, of whom a little over a third, 19,240, would lose their lives. It was to be a day like no other in British military history.

When attempting to describe the mood of the men of 1914–18 on going into battle, there is some case for differentiating between the Somme — in particular its catastrophic

61   1 July 1916, near Beaumont-Hamel, Somme: the firing of the Hawthorn Redoubt mine at 7.20 a.m., 10 minutes before zero. The premature explosion gave the Germans ample warning of the attack and they were ready for the British when they attacked. The battalion which advanced over this ground, the 16th Middlesex, lost 22 officers and 500 men. (Q754)

first phase — and the other major battles of the war. The effect of the Somme on the morale and attitudes of the British Army is a subject of continuing and often rancorous controversy. There are those who see the Somme battle as the tragic massacre of a generation, as an event so cataclysmic that it killed the breezy, crusading spirit of 1914–15 at a stroke and destroyed once and for all the grand, heroic view of war. This was when Siegfried Sassoon's 'happy legion' was happy no longer, when in the telling words of C. E. Montague — in a book whose title, *Disenchantment,* carries its own highly charged message — 'a web was woven across the sky and a goblin made of the sun'. There are others, however, who dismiss this interpretation as naïve, if romantic nonsense, exaggerated out of all proportion by the international acclaim that has surrounded for several decades the clique of young poets who most ardently expressed it. They claim that the British Army, despite the shattering defeat on the first day, came out of the Somme battle blooded, honed and confident, and that, by contrast, it was the German Army which had lost its cutting edge and its zest for battle. This is not the place to explore these arguments, each of which has its compelling pieces of evidence and its passionate expounders. It is sufficient for the purposes of this book that for many Saturday 1 July

1916 *was* a major watershed, and that there was among many battalions, particularly the amateur ones of Kitchener's Citizens' Army, an incontrovertible feeling that nothing would ever be the same again. (Ironically Kitchener had just died — drowned in HMS *Hampshire* off Orkney while on a mission to Russia — so that the chief inspirer of that Army was himself no more.) Lieutenant Robert Sutcliffe of the Bradford Pals could write of the forthcoming battle that it was 'a great thing to be in', but many of the New Army battalions were to be virtually annihilated on that dreadful first day, and the mood of the survivors was to be distinctly elegiac rather than heroic in retrospect. 'So ends a Golden Age' was the comment on that day by the official history of the 9th York and Lancasters, a Kitchener battalion which lost 423 men in its first battle. It also was the death-knell of the 'Pals' concept, since once the local nature of the unit was destroyed by heavy casualties there was no prospect of topping them up from the same source.

Before 1 July 1916, it was possible, if misguided, to believe that the Big Push would be the first step on the road to Berlin, that, in spite of the sinister warnings of Loos and Verdun, the Boche could be 'biffed' and beaten in one great show. After 1 July 1916 it became increasingly clear that the way would be long and hard and that the war would only be won at the cost of continuous and staggering losses. Before 1 July 1916 the new soldiers had only touched the fringes of war: they were now to experience it at its most savage.

All the accounts which follow in this chapter relate to that horrific first day. Ironically it was one of the most beautiful days of the war. Second Lieutenant Siegfried Sassoon wrote in his notebook that the weather 'was of the kind commonly called heavenly'. Bombardier R.H. Locke, Royal Horse Artillery, writing about it before the sixtieth anniversary of the battle, remembered it as a day without equal:

> It was really a pity to have a war on July 1st, for in all my time it was the most beautiful day we had. The sky was cloudless and the sun shone. The skylarks were singing as they flew heavenwards and unknown to them thousands of our soldiers were on their way there too.

Zero hour was 7.30. At 6.25, wrote Major Vignoles, Grimsby Chums, 'the artillery, which had been firing in a desultory manner, began to speed up, and within fifteen seconds there was a perfect hurricane of sound'. His account continues:

> We had an hour to wait, so lighted pipes and cigarettes while the men chatted and laughed, and wondered whether the Boche would wait for us. I had a look round but could not see much; the morning was fine and the sun shining, but the enemy trenches were veiled in light mist made worse no doubt by the smoke from the thousands of shells we were pumping into his lines. Nearby I could see our machine gunners, out in the open already, trying to get the best position from which to enfilade certain parts of the Boche line.
>
> There was a kind of suppressed excitement running through all the men as the time for the advance came nearer.

62   Waiting for 'zero hour'. 'How the time dragged on. Would it never come? At last. "One minute to go, get ready." Now for it, either death or glory, or pehaps a nice wound, good enough to get us across the water.' Corporal F.W. Billman (CO 873)

Vignoles himself did not go over with the first wave — and when he did attack he was almost immediately wounded — but in that short time he was able to see an infantry attack of the Great War in its most classic form:

> The mist had lifted slightly, and the picture before me, combined with the uproar, gave me an impression which I am not likely to forget.
>
> Looked at broadly, there was nothing horrible about it; the ground fell from where I was into Sausage Valley, rising again beyond covered with enemy trenches. No shells were falling on these, as our barrage had lifted, but dark green figures could be seen moving forward on the right, while No Man's Land was littered with men apparently lying down. At first it was difficult to realize that these were all casualties, and that what was left of the Battalions had pushed on.

Sausage Valley was a name given by the troops to a depression just to the right (looking towards the enemy lines) of La Boisselle, so named because it was frequently graced by a German observation balloon: predictably, there was a Mash Valley on the left. Both became places of carnage in the 1 July attack.

Dark figures moving forward, other figures lying down — all seen from such a distance that the horror of what was actually taking place was quite disguised. But what was it like to be one of those far-off figures?

63   *Second Lieutenant Roland
      Ingle, killed in action,
      7.45 a.m., 1 July 1916.
      Ingle's C.O. wrote in his
      letter of consolation: 'At the
      time when Roland was killed
      he was attached to a Trench
      Mortar Battery. All the
      TMBs were unable to get
      much beyond the front line, so
      intense was the German
      machine-gun fire . . . The fire
      that officers and men had to
      face in this b ttle was terrible,
      and your son led his men
      through it till he fell.'
      (Mrs Catherine Thackray)*

Second Lieutenant Kenneth Macardle was in the attack on Montauban, several miles to the south east, at precisely the same time that Major Vignoles was watching the attack on La Boisselle. His account forms one of the striking entries that fill the final pages of this remarkable young officer's diary:

> All around us and in front men dropped or staggered about; a yellow mass of lyddite shrapnel would burst and a section of men in two-deep formation would crumple up and be gone. We advanced in artillery formation at a slow walk. We led our sections in and out of the stricken men who were beyond help or whom we could not stop to help; it seemed callous but it was splendid war. Men crawling back smiled ruefully or tried to keep back blood with leaky fingers. We would call a cheery word or fix our eyes on Montauban — some men were not good to see.

In spite of the high casualties, this attack on Montauban was going well — too well, for Macardle's 17th Manchesters had to wait for 40 minutes under heavy shell-fire before they rushed the village at the assigned time of 9.56. By the time they moved forward 'A' Company was all but wiped out; their Sergeant-Major was killed, and only one officer was on his feet and he had been wounded. Macardle's 'B' Company came up with him as he ordered the survivors of his stricken company forward:

64   *Men of the Wiltshire Regiment going over the top to attack Thiepval during a later stage of the Somme Battle. Thiepval, a target of the first day, was finally taken in late September. (Q1142)*

> I caught a glimpse of young Wain, his face haggard with pain, one leg soaked with blood, smoking a cigarette and pushing himself forward with a stick. His voice was full of sobs and tears of pain and rage. 'Get up you ————s! Blast your souls — get up!' I waved to him and he smiled and dropped — he knew it was not absolutely up to him any longer. We of 'B' Company took over. We were enfiladed from our left (where another Battn had failed to advance) by machine guns and rifle fire, but we took the village from a fleeing and terror-struck enemy. The village was by then a monstrous garbage heap of stinking dead men and high explosives.

Private Henry Russell, 5th Battalion London Regiment, went over with the first wave at Gommecourt. He was very badly wounded, became one of countless figures 'lying down' in No Man's Land throughout that long summer day and was subsequently invalided out of the Army. It was to be many years before he felt himself able to write an account of what happened to him on 1 July 1916. He and his comrades of the 56th London Division began their advance under a heavy smoke screen; but then they found themselves beyond the smoke screen and they became an easy target for the German machine-guns:

During our advance, I saw many of my colleagues drop down, but this somehow or other did not seem to worry me, and I continued to go forward until I suddenly became aware that there were few of us in this first line of attack capable of going on. At this stage I found myself in the company of an officer, Lieut Wallace. We dived into a flat shallow hole made by our guns, apparently both wanting to decide what we should now do . . . I came to the conclusion that going on would be suicidal, and that the best thing we could do would be to stay there and attempt to pick off any Germans who might expose themselves. Lieut Wallace said, however, that we had been ordered to go on at all costs and that we must comply with this order. At this, he stood up and within a few seconds dropped down riddled with bullets. This left me with the same problem and, having observed his action, I felt that I must do the same. I, therefore, stood up and was immediately hit by two bullets and dropped down.

I must say that this action had a profound effect on me in later years. I had thought that a man who could stand up and knowingly face practically certain death in these circumstances must be very brave. I found out that bravery hardly came into it. Once the decision was made to stand up I had no further fear. I was not bothered at all even though I believed that I would be dead within seconds and would be rotting on the ground, food for the rats the next day. I did not even feel appreciably the bullets going through and this was to me something extraordinary. I am now convinced that when it comes to the last crunch nobody has any fear at all; it is not a question of bravery. In some extraordinary manner the chemistry of the body anaesthetizes it in such a way that even when fully conscious fear does not enter into the matter.

The worst experience I had was sometime later after I had crawled into another shell-hole some distance away and into which another colleague of mine had also crawled. He told me that he had been shot through the middle of the back and that the bullet had emerged through his left ear . . . We had not long to wait before a shell burst on the edge of our hole; it killed my colleague and injured me in such a way that I was virtually emasculated. I considered the situation hopeless and that even if a miracle happened and I did, in fact, get away, I would not be fit for anything in this world. I, therefore, decided to kill myself.

To this end, I was under the impression that I had three choices. The first was to explode a Mills bomb which I was carrying in my pocket. This seemed to be a silly procedure because it would only be doing what the Germans were already attempting to do. The second was to take a very large dose of morphine tablets which I believed to be in my pocket. Some time before, I had buried a doctor killed in action and on going through his belongings I had found a tube containing a considerable number of morphine tablets. I intended to take all these but when I felt in my breast pocket, I found that they were no longer there and somehow or other I had lost them. The third course was one which came to my mind as a result of a talk given to us by the Medical Officer before going into action. He said that, if wounded or bleeding, we should never take intoxicants, as the result would almost certainly be fatal. Before the attack I had bought a very large bottle of Worcester Sauce or Yorkshire Relish at an advanced NAAFI, emptied out the contents and filled it to the brim with rum. I therefore managed to get hold of the bottle of rum which I had put in my haversack and I drank the lot hoping that it would result in my death. In fact it did me no harm at all. It probably made me slightly merry and bright and rather stupified. It also probably caused me to drop off to sleep, though I am not aware of this. However, I came to the conclusion, when I had recovered my senses, that, in spite of my condition (my left arm being torn, my left thigh damaged, my right leg wounded and strips of flesh hanging down from my abdomen) it was still worth while making a serious effort to save myself.

Russell had to wait until 11 p.m. before he dared to make a move. He was found the following morning, when a Private of the Middlesex Regiment heard his feeble cries.

Even in those parts of the front where the battle had gone well — the extreme right wing of the attack, where the British had attacked side by side with five divisions of the French Army — men knew that they had been in a hard and historic fight. The remarkable Second Lieutenant Macardle, doyen of No Man's Land, devotee of 'splendid war', felt a touch of war-weariness as he and his fellow Manchesters sat it out in captured Montauban under the bombardment of the German guns. He wrote in his diary:

> We got tired of the shock of their explosions making us reel and feel dizzy and numbed: we got sick of the reek of high explosives which is synonymous with dead and broken men; our cheery triumphant treatment of those most unpleasant situations changed. When the first day and a night were gone we were silent and grim and — yes — a little afraid.

By way of a postscript to this chapter, it should be stated that violence was inflicted as well as suffered on the first day on the Somme, and not always according to the accepted rules of war.

Private Arthur Hubbard, London Scottish, whose letter before the battle was quoted in the previous chapter, wrote a further letter on 7 July from a hospital in England, to which he had been sent with a Blighty wound. After describing the opening stage of the battle as 'a terrible sight that I shall never forget as long as I live', he went on:

> We had strict orders not to take prisoners, no matter if wounded, my first job was when I had finished cutting some of their wire away, to empty my magazine on 3 Germans that came out of their deep dugouts, bleeding badly, and put them out of their misery, they cried for mercy, but I had my orders, they had no feelings whatever for us poor chaps.

The killing of prisoners was a rare phenomenon of the war, but it undoubtedly took place. Sometimes it was an act of spontaneous anger in response to what might be described as 'battle rage'; as for example in the Second Battle of Ypres, an action fought in fury after the introduction into the culture of that much resented weapon, 'poison gas'. Sometimes it could be an act of private revenge; thus in the 1917 Battle of Messines two soldiers accused of killing prisoners in their care, on being asked why they did so, replied that the mother of one had been killed in an air raid, while the sweetheart of the other had died in the bombardment of Scarborough back in 1914. Occasionally thrusting commanders issued unambiguous orders on the subject; thus Lieutenant-Colonel Frank Maxwell VC DSO, writing in October 1916 during the later stages of the Battle of the Somme, concluded a farewell message to the 12th Middlesex with this resounding paragraph:

> Finally remember that the 12th 'Die-Hards' DO KILL, DON'T TAKE PRISONERS UNLESS WOUNDED and DON'T retire . . . and with this one 'DO' and two 'DON'TS', I wish all ranks 'Goodbye' and 'God speed'.

Such orders could be received with disbelief. Thus a conscript infantryman wrote in his diary in September 1918 before an attack:

> Detailed instructions were given; *one of which was that we were to take no prisoners.* I might add that this order was given by a man who was a coward himself, and certainly not an Englishman.

Such practices were clearly rare; indeed their very rarity could, in many cases, create a sense of revulsion when soldiers were ordered to do that which they instinctively felt to be against the rules.

In the case of Arthur Hubbard, the impact was long-lasting. He recovered physically after the first day on the Somme, but he did not do so mentally. He committed suicide in 1929, the official verdict at his inquest being that his death was the result of shell-shock. His family was convinced that the episode that above all brought about his disintegration was his carrying out of official orders on 1 July 1916. Thus in the end he was as much a victim of the Somme as the men he felt obliged to kill on that memorable historic morning.

---

[1] I am indebted to former Private John Anderson, 18th Bn Northumberland Fusiliers, for this story: he heard the original shout.

12 Into battle: 'The most horrible invention that was ever known'

Acting Captain Reginald Leetham, 2nd Battalion Rifle Brigade, saw the Big Push of 1 July 1916 from the close vantage point of a battalion whose attack was cancelled at the eleventh hour because of the fate of the battalions that had gone before. He described his reactions to the battle in a brief but vivid diary. He realized from the moment he heard the rattle of machine-gun bullets overhead that 'fellows in the open must be being mowed down like grass'; and that day he saw three battalions practically annihilated. He wrote: 'They went into a greater hell and a worse valley of death than the gallant 600 the poem was written about.' He summed up his attitude in a series of brief, bitter paragraphs:

> I wonder if a Corps Commander eight miles behind the front line has any idea of what life is like in the front line.
>
> A modern battle is the most horrible invention that was ever known and as the war goes on each one gets worse . . .
>
> If we had heroes in previous wars, today we have them not in thousands but in half millions.

The previous chapter brought together a number of experiences all related to that one day which so appalled Captain Leetham and which had begun with such high hopes, the first day of the Battle of the Somme. In this chapter are collected a number of accounts of other actions scattered through the war, all of them subsequent to the great catastrophe of 1 July.

Broadly speaking, the writers are men, like Leetham, who have seen the face of battle and recognized it for what it is. 'War,' it has been said, 'was found out on July 1st', and certainly there is little emphasis on war as a superior form of ball-game or as some grand charade in which paper men faced painless deaths. There is even, as for example in Lance-Corporal Roland Mountfort's description of an attack on Pozières, a positive disclaimer of the jaunty, cavalier attitudes of 1 July — and the attack he was involved in took place only 15 days later!

> We moved off in platoons, overland, towards the front line. Then came the order to advance and before we knew where we were we were 'going over the top'. In the distance — a fearful way it seemed — was Pozières: and by now we were attacking it. Then the crumps began and what proved our undoing, machine guns crackled from the village. We advanced at the walk. There was a

65   *Guillemont after its capture in September 1916. Wrecked trees, wrecked German strong point.
A typical landscape of the later stages of the Somme battle. (Q1158)*

good deal of shouting — 'Keep up', 'don't bunch'. 'Half left' and so on, but
only necessary orders. We didn't dribble footballs, neither did we say 'This way
to Berlin, boys' nor any of the phrases employed weekly by the *News of the
World*.

Yet a caveat must be entered: the disenchantment caused by 1 July 1916 was by no
means universal. For many it was simply the beginning of a new challenge. Now that war
had been recognized it had to be lived with and mastered. Above all the German must be
made to know that 1 July was a temporary aberration only. Britain had suffered a bloody
nose; the next bloody nose would be the enemy's. And, for some, war could still be
enjoyable. It is significant that one of the most vivid accounts in this chapter relates to the
beginning of the Third Battle of Ypres, launched 13 months after the opening of the
Somme, and that the writer, a Guards Lieutenant, Alex Wilkinson, could still talk of battle
as 'splendid fun'. More, it is worth adding that this same young officer could write, in a
letter written only five days before the Armistice, that a battle in which he had fought was
'the best that I have ever had, and I would not have missed it for anything'.

The truth is, surely, that we are dealing with many men in many situations, and that each man reacted according to character and circumstance and in tune with the men around him. Equally understandably, some, simply by virtue of their character and personality, saw nothing particularly extraordinary in the new brutal form of war, and accepted it, horrors and all, and even exulted in killing; others, no less brave, found it so utterly inhuman that they felt moved to protest, disenchantment and, sometimes, despair.

Over the years the latter view has won a hands-down victory in the public mind. Now the vision of the Great War accepted by most people is of doomed battalions going endlessly over the top to perish hopelessly in mud, of men who died 'as cattle'. Some of the war's long-lived survivors came to accept that interpretation, but others retained the more positive, upbeat attitude which many held at the time, while it should also be said that an increasing number of serious students and historians have come to accept that disillusion was far from general even when conditions were at their worst. Both views, I believe, must be respected.

Captain Lionel Ferguson, 13th Battalion Cheshire Regiment, went into battle on the Somme front on 7 July 1916. There were no forecasts of easy success; in fact his battalion was promised 'a hard fight with much bayonet work'. As they marched towards the front line Ferguson became aware that a fellow officer was in a very bad state of nerves:

> I was marching at the back of No. 3 Coy, walking with Freddy Hall in charge of No. 4 Coy: his manner was very strange. He certainly felt the strain too much for him, also he had 'wind up', telling me he thought it would be his last show. He was killed next day.

Ferguson himself was far from being in command of his own emotions:

> With nobody to talk to, as Freddy was now speechless, I had to keep my thoughts from getting the better of me. I confess now I was very frightened. Sweat kept running down my face and neck. I could have drunk the sea dry: also a lump in my throat seemed to nearly stop my breathing. I tried to talk and words failed me, in fact no condemned man could have felt worse.

However, when the moment of the attack came he had mastered himself, in spite of the fact that he knew his battalion was 'going over the top of a square held on three sides by the enemy' and that 'those who had better ideas of "stunting" than I had were very pessimistic about the show'. Zero hour was preceded by an intense half-hour bombardment, which produced a heavy enemy reply:

> All sorts of dirt was flying about now and we had to lie very low to avoid being hit. The rim of my hat was punctured also a brick fell on it which thoroughly put the wind up me. My heart was once again in my mouth, but this time I knew I had complete self-control . . . I had a few old hands round me, as I was taking a platoon over, and they kept me cheery. One man in particular was fine, keeping us all laughing by his wit. We gave out a good rum ration at 7.30 and it did us a power of good, as the waiting to go over is most unnerving work. I

kept calling out the time. Five, four, three, two, one more minute to go. 'Over the top and the best of luck.' The barrage lifted and we were up to our front line before we knew it; but here we got it hot, Stewart in charge of no. 1 platoon was killed outright, the best officer in the battalion. I saw him a few moments later, quite dead, his lighted pipe still between his teeth. The Hun now could be seen all round, he had MGs mounted on 3 sides of us, it seemed as if our barrage had been ineffective. From this point we were just mown down. My blood was up, now my fear had gone and I wanted to kill and rushed on. Col Finch I saw in the middle of No Man's Land, trying to direct No. 1 Coy who now seemed to have lost direction. It appeared all their officers were hit and he called to me to get on and lead them to the enemy machine guns, now doing so much havoc. I did my best and with my batman Brown ran up forward. I felt a pain in my shoulder and found my arm was useless. I did not realize I was hit but fell headlong into a shell hole. Brown following, beginning to tie up with a bandage. I remember telling him off and began to fire at the MG crew, now not 30 yards away. Of course, I never hit them, but I kept seeing them fall, and quite had the idea it was my work. I must say I admired them, for no sooner than the man who was working the gun was hit, then another took his place on the seat of death; in fact, they seemed endless. At this point Brown was hit with a shrapnel ball in his cheek; it settled under his skin, giving him the appearance of having toothache: but I had to tie him up, and he informed me he was going back. Myself I did not want to go, but he said I was badly hit and was losing a lot of blood; this I could not see as it was running down my back. I was beginning to feel weak also, so decided to try and get back. We started by running, but after two falls, I rested in a shell hole. Brown ran on, getting safely into our old front line, from which he beckoned me to follow; I had fifty yards to go, and the ground all round was being torn by bullets, so I had grave doubts about doing it, but beginning to feel faint, and not wishing to be lying out I started to roll from hole to hole; in time reaching the trench.

Ferguson and Brown made their way back to the dressing station along with the other walking wounded, passing many 'awful sights' on the way:

> It was a long walk and I was getting weaker and my mind was wandering. I would talk to the troops who were going up: telling them what to do and what we had done. At last we arrived in Albert and entered a large hall filled with wounded. I saw Captain Dean getting a dressing put on and other friends lying dead and dying: the sight was so cruel that my nerve went and I fell down on the floor and started sobbing. I had had no sleep and little food for 60 hours, also was weak from loss of blood, so had some excuse.

Ferguson's wound took him home to Blighty. So too did the wound sustained by Second Lieutenant Blake O' Sullivan, 6th Battalion Connaught Rangers, during the attack

*66   Bringing in a badly wounded man after the capture of Guillemont, September 1916.
(Q4175)*

on Guillemont on the Somme in September 1916. He wrote his account of the action
from hospital in Chelsea in response to questions from his mother about the recent
fighting in France. He had had a hard introduction to war; there had been many casualties
before the battalion had any chance of engaging the enemy. He had even been showered
with the 'wet dust' of the blood and brains of a man standing next to him in a dugout
entrance, and had seen the battalion MO go mad with shell-shock:

> Sitting here in my hospital bed my mind is obsessed by the shocks and sights
> and the sudden deaths of so many friends during those last awful days. By
> writing down all the details I hoped to exorcise some of the mental migraine.

Waiting for zero hour, wrist-watch in hand, 'uneasily wishing for 12.03 to break the
horrible apprehension', he had glanced at the waiting men and found it hard to avoid 'a
morbid anxiety about their chances of surviving the coming hour'. But fortunately 'the
waves of sickening fear' which had plagued him at various intervals during the morning
had vanished. With the cacophony of the barrage around them and a piper 'blowing as if
his cheeks would burst — though, pathetically, nothing could be heard of the pipes above
the screeching din' — the Rangers went over the top and 'astounded me by a concerted

67   *A typical sight during a battle:*
      walking wounded hobbling back for
      medical attention. (Q6540)

yell and cheer that could be heard even above the bombardment'. As the attack began, 'for me the surrounding frenzy gave the illusion of taking place in the midst of a raging ocean tempest: and going over the top, like running shivering into ice-cold water'. There was the inevitable, ferocious German response:

> On the ridge we were greeted by a hurricane of machine gun bullets sounding like hosts of bees, whistling, swooshing and shrieking past our heads with blood-curdling intensity. What saved those cheering men from wholesale and instant death was the lucky miracle that the Boche fire was aimed a few feet too high. Coming over that high ground we presented such a perfect target that by rights not a soul should have escaped. I started by leading them towards the quarries; but, suddenly seeing Tamplin's Company attacking the concrete strong point, veered and headed for that. The pulverized ground was soggy, and the cheering faded in the heavy going while the charge slowed gradually into a laboured jog-trot. The constant need to skirt the constellation of shell-holes broke up our wave formation which soon looked more like a post-match mob invading a football field.
>
>   The bombardment crescendo reached its climax with the onset of an intense shrapnel umbrella (probably British, as we were minutes ahead of timetable). About 200 feet above us the air became stippled by swarms of brown-black

68   *An Australian Advanced Dressing Station working at full stretch during the Third Battle of Ypres Salient, September 1917. (E(AUS) 715)*

splashes as the shells burst and scattered hell in all directions. I glanced fearfully to right and left to see the effect of this new menace and was surprised to find that so many were still going strong, though here and there a man would suddenly huddle into a little bundle. Even as I watched a corporal close behind me pitched forward with arms stretched out and hands clutching frantically at the mud. We were already within a few yards of the looming strong point and still saw nothing of the enemy. The great concrete block was unscathed by all the strafing and two slits in each wall glowered at our onrush like cynical eyes. Some of D Company stood to one side of the loopholes in the north wall and tried unsuccessfully and dangerously to lob grenades through the slits. Guessing there'd be some sort of entrance at the back I spurred myself for a final rush to get round to it from the south side, dashed past one of the west wall eyes and suddenly felt a terrific thump and a streak of burning pain across the shoulders: stumbled on for a few paces, tripped over some wire and fell flat on my face and realized that a bullet had got me.

I dragged myself and rifle to a shallow hole to assess the wound. Spit on my hands showed no blood from lung damage and only the shoulders and back hurt badly — though arms weighed like lead.

69   *Severely wounded Canadians awaiting evacuation in a motor ambulance, July 1917.*
      (CO 1636)

Looking along the wave I was aghast to see that my fall had been misinterpreted as a taking of cover. Everyone was doing likewise; even CSM Johnson close left was crawling into a convenient shell hole. In a frenzy I got up and shrieked myself hoarse but to no purpose. To signal with my arms was painful and slow, but by dragging the rifle by its muzzle and going forward at least indicated that the advance should go on. Moments later they were all up and going again.

The unrehearsed breather was a lucky chance, because once on their feet the men recovered the wild abandon of the charge just at the moment when the Germans began to emerge from shell holes and wrecked trenches. Behind the strong point a scuffle and scramble developed as a group put up a hectic resistance that was overwhelmed by the bayonet-stabbing onslaught; a vortex of shrieking; of yells and brutish grunting — then rushing ahead, leaving the crumpled bodies in a stink of blood and high explosive. Some idiot exploded his p-bomb on my right front and a phosphorous cloud swept over and obliterated the shambles. Choking, and blasting the careless fool who had blinded and almost smothered me, I staggered out of the smoke. By the time my eyes cleared the tide of men had swept on and was already into the heart of Guillemont.

70   Army Form B 104-81A: the standard
      form by which next-of-kin were
      informed when a soldier was wounded.
      (IWM Department of Documents)

Private Albert Johnson, 11th Battalion Royal West Kents, was in the successful infantry attack that followed the blowing of 19 mines under the German front-line trenches in the vicinity of Messines in the early morning of 7 June 1917. As compared with the standard situation on the Somme resistance was minimal and by the end of the day the British had reached and held the German second line. Private Johnson wrote an account of his part in the battle in a letter of 10 June. For a long time he had been fascinated to know what being in action was really like:

> I remember that whilst in England last year I read with active interest the first
> account of the Battle of the Somme and tried to get my mind to imagine what
> a push was like but now having had the personal experience I realize the
> impossibility of it. Waiting for the word for up and over I began to feel a trifle
> dozy but this speedily vanished when the mines went up. Our trench rocked
> like a ship in a strong sea and it seemed as if the very earth had been rent
> asunder. We started for Fritz and the land he occupied which is better known
> as the Ridge. What passed in that journey across No Man's Land was only a
> passing vision of moving figures intent on gaining their objective pausing only
> for a breather in a shell hole, for the vicinity was as if an earthquake had passed
> over it so great had been the havoc wrought by our splendid artillery. On we
> went until we came across our first opposition — a machine-gun which began
> to spit very nasty from our extreme left. From this whilst lying in a shell hole

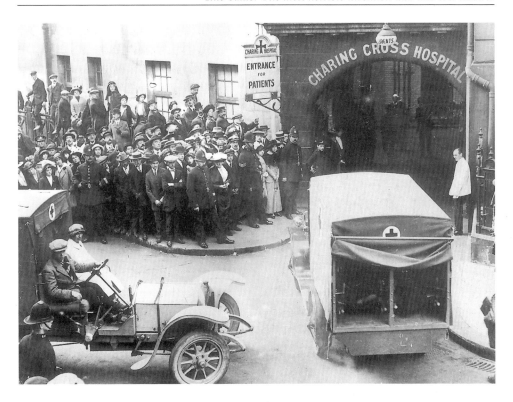

71 *Wounded from the Western Front arriving at Charing Cross Hospital, London; a scene recorded in September 1914 but repeated throughout the war. What Lance-Corporal Roland Mountfort called 'the fatheaded crowd' is present, as always when train loads of wounded were expected. (Q53275)*

I had my first reminder, a bullet hitting the earth four or five inches in front of me which sent the dirt flying, in my face. Eventually the difficulty was overcome but I cannot vouch what became of gun or Germans.

There was a pause in the attack while they were waiting for the barrage to lift. Johnson took advantage of the lull to move to a more advantageous position:

But before I could reach my objective one of Fritz's shrapnel shells came over and burst immediately in front of me but for some unaccountable reason two of my comrades passed between it and me and therefore caught the full force of the burst while I was extremely fortunate only to get my right ear peppered. I found I was bleeding but not feeling anything I took no notice of it and carried on. We came to a wood where Fritz began to appear in large numbers. His morale was badly shaken however and he had no stomach for a fight and they threw equipment right and left and ran out towards us as hard as they could in order to get out of our barrage which had properly put the wind up them.

Lieutenant Alex Wilkinson, 2nd Battalion Coldstream Guards, went into action on the first day of the Third Battle of Ypres, 31 July 1917. Exhilarated, content with his and his battalion's performance, he wrote in a letter to his father a breezy account of the opening phase of what was to become the great set-piece battle of the third year of the war. He went into the attack with one extra advantage: a complete confidence in the certainty of his own survival (see Chapter. 9), though soon men were falling quite near him:

> A 5.9 pitched within about 5 yards of my leading half platoon, killing two and wounding one: two such good fellows. I heard this shell coming and saw it just before it pitched. If I had been on the right instead of the left of my platoon it must have had me. All I could do was curse the Hun and carry on.

As the attack developed his Company Commander was wounded, Wilkinson confidently took over:

> Away we went reaching our final objective at 9.25. We were supposed to be there at 9.23! Arrived there, it was an imaginary line right in the open. I ascertained that the company was in line, the flanks secure etc., and then we dug in. It was at this juncture that we suffered most. Snipers were very active and several men were hit and then before we could get a proper line dug a Hun aeroplane came over and spotted us, with the result that we were immediately crumped and rather heavily, suffering further casualties. Eventually we got a fairly good line dug, linking up shell holes etc., and there we stayed . . . I could tell you heaps more, various incidents, but I have given you a fair idea of the war side of it. The war side of it was splendid fun, we all enjoyed it immensely, but the weather side of it was very different. I never thought the human frame could endure such hardships.

The weather Lieutenant Wilkinson referred to in his letter was to be a persistent belligerent in the third battle of Ypres and to bedevil the British chances of success. This was its first strike:

> At 6 p.m. the night we arrived at our objectives it began to rain and continued incessantly for 30 hours. In a proper line of trenches it would have been quite beastly, but in an absolutely new line with practically no means of revetting it, it beggars description.

They had more than 48 hours to go before they came out of the line followed by an 'awful walk back', but morale could not have been higher:

> Never for a moment did the men lose heart. No men, even of the original expeditionary force, could have done better. The only thing they wanted was a chance to kill more Huns. They were rather too quick on our front: we couldn't see them for dust. It is said that no Huns can be induced to face the

Guards Division and it looks like it. They knew we were coming! The men were praying for a counter attack and so was I, for then we could have fairly slaughtered them!

Battle murdered men but it also murdered landscape and destroyed villages and towns. Men were often deeply moved by what would now be called the 'collateral' damage of war and responded accordingly. Of the three comments that follow two relate to the battlefield of the Somme while the third relates to the much battered 'capital' of the Ypres Salient, Ypres city itself.

As far as you can see is a wilderness of torn up soil intersected with ruined trenches: it is like a man's face after small pox or a telescopic view of the moon. The shell holes overlap and run into each other; some are mere scratches, some would hide an average haystack; here and there a few distorted posts form all that remain of a barbed wire entanglement. But the most startling feature is the debris that is lying scattered on the surface and thick in the trenches. Sets of equipment, rifles, bayonets, shovels, shrapnel helmets, repirators, shell cases, iron posts, overcoats, groundsheets, bombs (in hundreds) — I don't suppose there is a square yard without some relic and reminder of the awful waste of war.

Lance Corporal Roland Mountfort, 10th Bn Royal Fusiliers, July 1916

The woods had changed hands by repeated German counter attacks and shelling and it had been difficult to bury the dead. The trees were criss-cross, with shattered, splintered limbs, and the stench was awful, and we could hardly put a pick in the ground or shovel but what we would strike a buried body and clothing. The ground was pock-marked with shell holes everywhere and one place we found a whole machine-gun team buried by shell fire.

Tom Macdonald, 9th Bn Royal Sussex Regt, August 1916

Would that every brick and stone there [Ypres] could be swallowed up in the earth tomorrow, if that would help us to forget what they have seen! Those narrow streets of ruins, the crumpled water-tower, the daredevil prison standing up there until it should be knocked down; the dingy cellar where we played the gramaphone; the mangled bodies of those two officers who were killed in the street outside the door that afternoon; the abandoned switch canal all covered with long weeds; and, leaning miserably over all, the gaunt, maimed cathedral tower and Cloth Hall, left to be as great a mockery of civilization as the world will ever see. I suppose that men will flock to see the ghastly remains of that city. Let them walk with reverent and humble step.

Major R.S. Cockburn, 10th Bn Royal Rifle Corps

72   *Poison Gas, first used by the Germans on 22 April 1915, at Ypres, helped to produce some of the most haunting images of the war. British troops in anti-phosgene masks manning a Vickers machine-gun on the Somme front in July 1916. (Q3995)*

73   *There were many types of gas: chlorine, phosgene, chloropicrin, mustard, prussic acid, tear gas. The men in this photograph, dated 10 April 1918, at an Advanced Dressing Station near Béthune, are suffering from tear gas: this caused temporary blindness. (Q11586)*

13 'The terrible price'

Somewhere in Flanders.
19:7:16

Dear Ernest,
Thanks muchly for your letter d/12:7:16. So pleased to hear that you have landed home again, also that you are going on well.

Sergeant E.E. Lane, in hospital in England after being wounded in France, received a letter from a fellow Sergeant of the 6th Battalion of the Royal Berkshire Regiment, telling him how his battalion and its various members had fared on the Somme:

You remember that morning, I waited on the road for over an hour for the Ambulances, first one I saw was Sergt Thomas poor chap. I think he was pretty hard hit on the right shoulder, his jacket was pretty red I noticed, hope he is nicely tucked up somewhere in hospital. I heard from Medcraft, another of my chums, the other day, he is in Reading no. 4 War Hospital. If you would care to write to him, poor old chap, 'can't sit down', what a pity. But still, he's far away from Shrapnel and the like . . .

I am very pleased to say that both Woodley and Hawkins two more of my pals came out with a whole skin; Woodley brought Mr Brown, one of our Officers, back with him, he was badly wounded in both legs and arms, poor chap has since died. We lost Mr Haywood my Platoon Officer and Mr Child missing, and the Captain badly wounded. I hear he has since died. I am so sorry, although we had only had him with us a week or two. I am sure every man thought a lot of him. We had quite a number wounded in my platoon. Haycock, Wylde, England, Bullen, Wyles, Wood, Osborne, House, Nash, Robinson. Missing: L/Cpl Hilsdon my best pal, Pte Webb, Giles, Hudson, L/Cpl Searies. Pte Morgan killed. Corpls House and Tucker are missing and quite a number of L/Cpls and men of other platoons . . .

Well now old chap, keep smiling and you'll get well again, kindest regards, all kind thoughts and good wishes, to you from us all, I will always remain,
Your Chum, Ivern Deacon.

74   *A dead British soldier in a trench at Guillemont, Somme, September 1916; an image which refutes the assumption that official photographers only took pictures of enemy dead. (Q3964)*

22nd July, 1916
My dear Hall,
I do hope you will not think me unkind or neglectful that I have not written to you before. Believe me, I have often thought of you, and have been living in hopes of hearing how you are getting on.

Captain H.S.H. Hall, 10th Battalion Royal Fusiliers, lost an eye in his battalion's attack on Pozières in mid July 1916. In hospital in England, he received a letter from his Commanding Officer Lieutenant-Colonel the Hon. Robert White:

First, let me thank you from the bottom of my heart for your splendid and gallant conduct, and for the glorious example of duty you set the men. Your loss is irreparable to me. I can only hope and trust that you may be spared pain and soon restored to health and to your family. You deserve all the rest and happiness that I hope is in store for you . . .
Well, we have paid a terrible price! Though very sad, I am filled with pride

at the bearing of the dear 10th. Poor Taylor and Bevir are gone, as you know. Dear little Haviland died at Heilly on the 16th very badly wounded. Heathcote followed him next day and they lie quite close to each other and not far from poor Hodding, who died on the 10th. To my great grief our dear Shurey died yesterday, and we all went over to his funeral in the same graveyard as the others, about 400 yards from the railway station and under a beautiful hanging wood. I am grateful to think that they were all nursed by nice English nurses, and tended by good surgeons.

Richards you know was also killed, poor fellow . . .

We are an attenuated little band. We lost 397 K. and W. in the two days, but full of cheer; doing our best to re-organize and hope to have another go at the Bosch soon. In General Orders the Battalion and Brigade were complimented. The message ran —'the 10th did all that gallant British soldiers could do'!

Do let me hear how you are getting on and where you are. I miss you sadly, but am very proud to have had such officers and men under me. God bless you! Every kind wish.

Your grateful Colonel,
Robert White.

P.S. I watched your grand advance from the Chalk Pit on the road.

Such letters move as much by their list of names of the wounded and fallen as by the circumstances they describe. Second Lieutenant Kenneth Macardle, writing on 6 July, in what was to prove the last entry in his eloquent diary, mourned the loss of his friends who had fallen in the attack on Montauban five days earlier:

All the world is forever dead to Vaudrey, Kenworthy, Chesham, Sproat, Ford, and of the 'other ranks' we do not know how many. Vaudrey used to love rousing parades; Chesham had loved to hunt the buck in Africa when the heat was shimmering with the birth of a day . . . Young Victor was killed — his problem of marriage to a woman six years senior to him finally settled. Towers Clark is dead and Captain Law of County Down . . . We are about 400 strong tonight — we who went in 800.

One of the most famous tragedies of 1 July was that which overtook the 36th (Ulster) Division as a consequence of its great attack in the vicinity of Thiepval. Brilliantly successful at first, penetrating deep into enemy ground, the advance could not be sustained owing to the relative failure of the divisions to its right and left. Thus exposed, the division suffered massive casualties on a scale which would leave a permanent sense of grief in the province of Ulster. One immediate consequence was the following letter by a young, unsophisticated soldier of the division, Herbert Beattie of the 2nd Battalion Royal Inniskilling Fusiliers. Stunned by the deaths of so many comrades, Fusilier Beattie wrote home; again there is that moving litany of names:

75   *The military cemetery at Heilly, just behind the battlefield of the Somme, where Havilland, Heathcote, Hodding and Shurey, all young officers of the 10th Royal Fusiliers, lie buried (see the letter by Lieutenant-Colonel Robert White). The photograph shows the cemetery as it was in December 1916. (E(AUS) 42)*

Dear Mother,

Just a few lines to let you know I am safe and thank God for it, for we had a rough time in the charge we made. Mother don't tell V. Quinn's mother or Archer's (mother) that they must be killed (or) wounded for they are missing from roll-call, and tell Hugh that the fellow who used to chum about with E. Ferguson, called Eddie Mallon (he used to keep pigeons if Hugh does not know him, McKeown knows him) has been killed. Tell them that there is not another Grosvenor Road fellow left but myself. Mother, we were tramping over the dead; I think there is only about four hundred left out of about 13 hundred. Mother, you can let Alfred know something about all this. Mother, I have some German helmets and sausages, and I am sorry that I could not send them home. Mother, if God spares me to get home safely, I will have something awful to tell you. If hell is any worse I would not like to go to it. Mother, let me hear from you as soon as possible, as I have had no word from you this fortnight. Don't forget to let me hear from you soon

From your loving son Herbie[1]

76   *Not looting or searching for souvenirs, but retrieving identification papers and identity tag so that the dead soldier's details could be formally recorded. Château Wood, Ypres Salient, 1917. (E (AUS) 4599)*

Survivors withdrawing from the line after such an experience presented a grim spectacle, one distinctly sobering for those due to take their place. Captain Lionel Ferguson, 13th Battalion Cheshire Regiment, moving up on 3 July; saw the remainder of a Highland division coming out:

> It was a sight new to me to see really tired men, they were just walking along in twos and threes, holding each other up for support, unshaven, covered with mud, and war-worn, in fact never have I seen troops in worse condition. I met with them Major Popham, whom I had known in Bebington days, he had now a staff job with that division. He was pleased to see me, but told me they had had an awful time and that they were a smashed division.

77 *Burial party bear Monchy-le-Preux, August 1918. Death was so common that men could become callous. Private Archie Surfleet wrote: 'We went out at night on a stretcher-bearing party. We first of all got in all the wounded we could find and scoured the whole area. I think it is creditable that every wounded man was brought in . . . There were dozens of dead bodies about; we collected all we could and stacked them in piles for removal to a decent burial further back. I am still amazed at the casual way we piled those bodies, like so many huge logs, without any horror at such a gruesome task; which seemed to show we must be getting hardened.' (Q23612)*

The paying of a 'terrible price' on the field of battle — in particular by those most vulnerable of fighting men, the infantry — was a commonplace of the Great War. It was not unknown for battalions to be virtually annihilated. On 1 July 1916 certain battalions lost over 90 per cent of their attacking strength in killed and wounded. Usually between 700 and 800 men went into battle: on the morning of 1 July — in a matter of minutes, though the full toll would not be known for some time — the 10th Battalion of the West Yorkshire Regiment sustained 710 casualties and the 1st Battalion of the Newfoundland Regiment 684 casualties. A sizeable proportion of every battalion, usually including a senior officer (often the second-in-command), was left behind in the safety of the base area, so that whatever happened its continuity could be maintained. But what guaranteed continuity could not guarantee continued identity. When men who had lived and trained together for many months marched into the savagery of a set-piece battle, there was the virtual certainty not only that there would be huge losses but that the unit with which they had come to identify themselves would never be quite the same again.

There would be numerous variations of the July experience as the Battle of the Somme ground on over the following months. Thus Captain Harry Yoxall, 18th Battalion King's Royal Rifle Corps, wrote the following letter to his 'Dearest Mater and All' from a rest camp after the heavy fighting on the Somme in mid-September:

> Our brigade took its part in the general operations of the 15th-17th. I cannot give you any details as yet; but we reached all our objectives and held them till relieved, advanced for over 1½ miles on a 500 yards frontage, captured a village and took 750 prisoners . . . But the cost was heavy. My own battalion was particularly unfortunate . . . Of those that one or other of you knows Major Fadd, Captains Lester and Langford are all killed. Each is a tragedy in himself. Fadd was the best of good fellows, an adored son and brother, and had had a meteoric career in the army. Then there is Lester's wife — poor girl, I can't bear to think of her. And Langford's only brother was killed at Ploegsteert last June.
>
> I can't give you details of casualties, but four other officers including the Colonel and the Adjutant, were killed and eight wounded.
>
> I am still heavy with lack of sleep and fortunately perhaps can't realize what has happened. It seems impossible that all these people with whom I have lived and worked for all these past months are no more — just washed out as far as we are concerned. But it is so: and all that we that are left can do is to set to and pull the depleted battalion together and make it once more what it was. For it was a good battalion: not brilliant but hardworking and dogged: so that though we had, under the terrible shell-fire, to give up our third objective once and retire through the village we came again and held it till relieved.

When a soldier lost his life, it was normal practice for someone in his battalion unit to write a letter of consolation to his next of kin. On 10 November 1915 Private Edgar Foreman, Civil Service Rifles, was killed during a routine spell in the trenches. Three days later Captain Arthur Roberts, officer in charge of 'D' Company (who would himself lose his life 10 months later) wrote to the dead man's father:

> Dear Sir,
> It is my painful duty to acquaint you of the death of your son killed in action on November 10th. He was killed together with two others by a shell and we buried all three together close by. There is little of comfort that I can add. Your son was a fine soldier, who always did his share and played his part cheerfully and well. He died doing his duty. It may provide you some small comfort to know that death was instantaneous: he suffered no pain. We all, officers and men, join with you in mourning his loss.

On 18 August 1916 Captain Goronwy Owen, 15th Battalion Royal Welsh Fusiliers, wrote to the widow of Private A.J. Salway:

78   *A burial service on the Western Front; Canadians paying last respects to a fallen comrade.*
(CO 879)

Dear Madam,

I regret that pressure of work and illness have prevented me from writing earlier to express my sympathy with you in the loss of your husband, who met his death while gallantly doing his duty in action.

He was engaged at the time in carrying water and rations to his comrades in the wood during the fighting. It was, indeed, a case of a man laying down his life for his comrades. His death was instantaneous and mercifully he suffered no pain.

All of us, officers and men, mourn his loss. He was a good and conscientious soldier and did his duty nobly and well. No better testimony could be given to any man.

We all offer you and your family our heartiest and sincerest sympathy. May God protect and comfort you and all that are near and dear to you.

When the fighting on the Somme was closed down in November 1916 Second Lieutenant Norman Collins, 1/6th Battalion Seaforth Highlanders, then aged 19, became burial officer in the Beaumont-Hamel sector. He superintended the burial of over a

79 *Some ceremonies were much more
    perfunctory. When his brother Alex was
    killed, Tom Macdonald was distressed to
    find that apart from himself the only ones
    present for the burial were 'the padre and
    officer and a grave digger. My brother
    was just sewn up in hessian sacking and
    the padre gave the service. My "bone"
    comes in my throat as I remember this
    and I can hardly write this but I feel I
    must for my sons and others to see the
    futility of war.' The photograph shows
    Private Alex Macdonald's grave, at
    Philosophe, near Lens. (Author)*

thousand men and wrote to many of the parents. He preserved some of the replies, including this letter from a bereaved mother:

> It was a great comfort to me to hear from you and to speak so highly of him and I know very well that it is for a good cause we are fighting. But if only his sweet young Life had been spared I cant realize he is gone and that I will never see him again. Well Dear Sir I hope and pray that you may get through all right and that your nearest and dearest may be spared the terrible blow that the sad news brings for it just breaks a Mother's Heart.
>
> I hope you will overlook the liberty I have taken in writing to you but I felt I must thank you.

'Death was instantaneous'; 'he suffered no pain . . .': almost invariably this ritualistic consolation was offered to the mourning relatives. It could, of course be true: many men were killed instantly by the bullet in the heart or brain or the sudden explosion of a shell. But there must have been countless times when this well-tried formula covered up a hideous and agonizing death. It was inevitable in such circumstances that reality should be softened by the admixture of a harmless fiction: what good would there be in telling the awful truth to a broken young widow or to grieving parents?

Death in fact was rarely tidy; rather it was ugly, degrading, dehumanizing. When Gunner Hiram Sturdy, Royal Field Artillery, saw his first death he found it an unforgettable experience:

I crouch in behind some infantry holes (I don't call them shelters) and while there, one of the infantry is carried in. The top of the head is lifted off, a clean swipe whatever got him. His chum holds his head and I see him die. The first for me to see die, as they say, for his country, and it might be glorious, noble, brave, heroic, and all the rest of these beautiful words that sound so well on a platform or toasting your toes by the fireside, but it certainly is not a glorious sight to see a young fellow, with his face covered with blood, stiffening out in a hole dug out of clay. It isn't glorious, it's murder, was my thoughts when I saw my first infantryman die, and the years which I have lived since have only lowered the glories to the lowest depths and raised 'war is murder' to the highest pinnacle.

The chum sits a little time looking at the bloody clay with a uniform on it, then buckles up, and goes out to the bloody war.

Second Lieutenant Blake O'Sullivan, 6th Battalion Connaught Rangers, was mapping the trenches which the battalion had just occupied on the Somme front in late August 1916 (prior to the attack on Guillemont described in the previous chapter) when he came across the body of one of their corporals, killed while coming up to the line the previous night:

He was on his back with one knee crooked up and arms thrown apart, looking for all the world like a weary hiker. A gold wedding ring gleamed on one slightly closed hand and I wondered what thieving ghoul would eventually take it. A dreadful cloud of flies came buzzing up from him and I hurried past without looking any closer.

Captain Reginald Leetham, 2nd Battalion Rifle Brigade, while engaged in tending the wounded of 1 July 1916, came across a trench into which corpses had been heaped:

The trench was a horrible sight. The dead were stretched out on one side, one on top of each other 6 feet high. I thought at the time I should never get the peculiar disgusting smell of the vapour of warm human blood heated by the sun out of my nostrils. I would rather have smelt gas a hundred times. I can never describe that faint sickening horrible smell which several times almost knocked me up altogether. To do one's duty, one was actually climbing over corpses in every position and when one trod on human flesh it sent a shudder down one's spine.

Of the hundreds of corpses I saw, I only saw one pretty one — a handsome boy called Schnyder of the Berkshires who lay on our fire step shot through his heart. I wish his mother could have seen him — one of the few whose faces had not been mutilated. His eyes were open and he had a smile on his face: I suppose he died with the pleasure of knowing he had done his duty. His hair had not been ruffled and, unlike me, he had recently had a shave. There were no terrors of death on his face, poor boy.

Captain Leetham was himself killed in action, on 12 October 1917.

Fortunately for the sanity of the survivors, the very scale of the slaughter seems to have produced its own anaesthesia. It was possible for men to look on the most terrible of sights, to hear the most appalling evidence of pain and suffering, and still carry on. Corporal F.W. Billman, 9th Battalion East Surrey Regiment, on 25 September 1915, found himself in the dark, in the rain and under shell-fire on the battlefield of Loos: it was his first taste of war. Around him

> the ground was sprinkled with dead and dying heroes, but we had no time to stop and look at them, and soon got used to the ghastly faces, more so after midnight, as the moon shone out brilliantly. Many lay as they fell, some in an easy position, and one actually had a letter in his hand, as though he had managed to read it through before he died.

Private Archie Surfleet, on 16 November 1916, spent a night collecting badly wounded from No Man's Land after a show which had produced many casualties. In his diary he wrote:

> Most of us have lost pals and some of them will never come back, but it is surprising how little 'brooding' there is about . . . The lists of killed and wounded seem unending: yet practically everyone seems to take it all in an almost uncanny calmness. We are all looking forward to better times: God knows we can do with them.

Mass deaths in an action were part of the job description, but there could be sudden one-off fatalities in quiet times and a psychological mechanism had to be found for such events too. Private Peter McGregor, 14th Battalion Argyll and Sutherland Highlanders, wrote to his wife in what would be his last letter in September 1916:

> One of our men was caught by a sniper — he was standing by the entrance to his dugout. I saw the stretcher which came along to take the poor fellow away. His passing didn't seem to cause much stir — crowds of chaps were standing about, of course we all came to attention as it passed that was all. The business of the hour had to go on. A dead man is no use to the army, get him out of the way as quickly as possible.
>
> War is a terrible thing, and so few people realize it.

McGregor's death was an equally casual one; he was killed when a random shell burst in the trench in which he was standing.

It is necessary to add, however, that the capacity to 'soldier on' in spite of the deaths of comrades should not necessarily be taken as a sign of indifference. 'When I think of my poor dear old chums who have fallen I could cry', wrote Private Jack Sweeney in a letter home of 1916: and he was expressing a widely held sentiment. More, the grief men suffered was, in many cases, permanent. Anyone who has spoken to a survivor of a 'Pals'

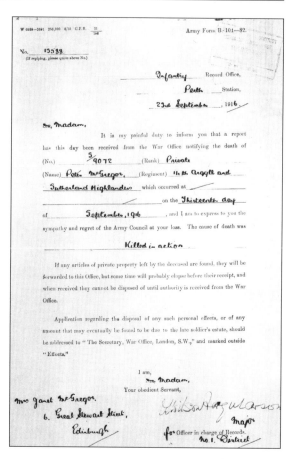

80, 81   Army Form B.101-82.

Official communication informing Mrs Janet McGregor of the death of her husband, Private Peter McGregor (pictured above), aged 44, 14th Battalion Argyll and Sutherland Highlanders, killed in action, 13 September 1916. In a letter to her his Company Commander wrote: 'We buried him last night in the British Military Cemetery. It was a beautiful evening and the simple service was held while the guns were booming round us. May the one who governs all sustain you and your family in your heavy loss. "Greater love hath no man than this, that he gave up his life for his friends".'

82   Peter McGregor's grave, at Maroc Cemetery, near Vermelles. (Shirley Seaton)

83 *Effects-Form 45B. Official letter of 6 March 1917 informing Mrs Annie Farlam that she was due the sum of £4, 1 shilling and 4 pence in settlement of the accounts of her late husband, Lance-Corporal Thomas Henry Farlam, Grenadier Guards, killed during a major offensive on the Somme, 16 September 1916. His body was not found; he thus became one of the 73,000 missing of the Somme battle.*

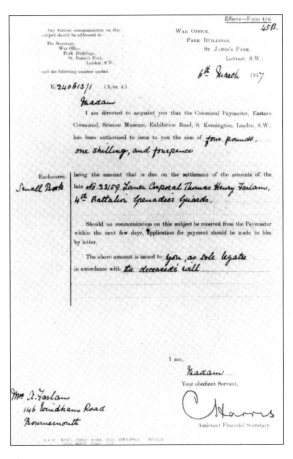

84 *Mrs Annie Farlam, a photograph retrieved from the 'small book' of her late husband, left behind when he went into action. It also contained her most recent letter to him, in which she had written: 'If this war does not stop soon I think every body will go mad. Hoping to hear from you soon with a Bit of News.'*

85   *Grave of an unknown British soldier, Thiepval, September 1916, a reminder that this war*
was remarkable for a huge number of unidentified dead in all the participating armies, a fact
which led directly to the postwar cult of the Unknown Warrior. (Q1540)

battalion, for example, will realize how deeply such a man could be moved at the thought
of his fallen comrades a virtual lifetime after their deaths.

One thing that could disturb that 'almost uncanny calmness' referred to by Private
Surfleet was an inability to cope with the agonies of the wounded. Death instantly put a
man in a separate category; he was beyond help; in Captain Yoxall's phrase, he was 'washed
out'. His body became instantly disposable, to be got under ground as soon as possible:
the basic niceties could follow later. The wounded were different. Captain Leetham of the
Rifle Brigade, after hours of attempting to help the survivors of the holocaust of 1 July
1916, wrote in his diary:

> It was the wounded that made the place such a Hell. I did not mind the dead.
> I could do nothing for them, but one felt so incapable of doing much for the
> wounded . . .
> Every now and then a wounded man crawled in. I shall never forget the

agony in their faces, especially towards midnight when some had been out for 16 hours.

Quite a number, for the time I hope, had gone stark staring mad . . .

Stretcher-bearers were frightfully scarce. What was the use of a handful of stretcher-bearers to deal with literally thousands of wounded. It was two o'clock in the afternoon before I saw a doctor. All I could do was to give brandy and water to men we rescued from being buried alive; also to men who had to lie for hours with broken legs I gave morphia. I got rid of two tubes of morphia and two big flasks of brandy.

Private Tom Macdonald, 9th Battalion Royal Sussex Regiment, had a similarly frustrating experience on a similarly hot summer's day on the Somme: 'The worst part was when we could not get badly wounded back. Some were screaming for water and we could only moisten their lips with jam.'

But when men *did* rescue a wounded comrade, there was a profound satisfaction. Private Surfleet was near Oppy Wood in May 1917 when he and his friends

noticed a chap stretched out on the strip of road, the Bailleul-Oppy road, which ran by the end of the bit of trench we were in. He waved an arm in our direction: Whole, Hurste, Bridge and I took a stretcher from the pile outside the MO's place and ambled along the road to him. Until we got right up to him we did not realize he must have been in full view of the enemy: he was just over the rise nearing Oppy Wood. We put him on the stretcher and brought him back to the Aid Post: he had been out there two days and nights with his leg shattered and had been trying to get back to our lines, using an old rifle as a crutch. I shall never forget that man's expression of gratitude when we got him safely to the shelter of the Aid Post: the tears in his eyes gave us an inkling of the hell he had been through. I know I had a peculiar feeling of exhilaration as he waved goodbye when the stretcher-bearers took him away.

Death and wounds were part of the standard fabric of war. But this conflict saw a new and frightening phenomenon: poison gas. Lance-Sergeant Elmer Cotton's company was attached to a South Lancs battalion for training in 1915 when they received orders to reinforce the line. On the way up they passed a dressing station:

Propped up against a wall was a dozen men — all gassed — their colours were black, green and blue, tongues hanging out and eyes staring — one or two were dead and others beyond human aid, some were coughing up green froth from their lungs — as we advanced we passed many more men lying in the ditches and gutterways — shells were bursting all around.

Then Cotton and his comrades came under a gas attack themselves. He had already been affected by a whiff of gas earlier in the day; this caused him to spit and he had to take off his respirator to clear his throat:

My respirator fell to pieces with the continual removal and readjustment — the gas closed my eyes and filled them with matter and I could not see. I was left lying in the trench with one other gassed man and various wounded beings and corpses and forced to lie and spit, cough and gasp the whole of the day in that trench.

Eventually he was evacuated by motor field ambulance to hospital:

That was a fearful day for the British — they sustained 3000 'gas' cases alone not to mention the wounded and dead due to shell-fire and rifle and machine-gun bullets.

The inevitable result of all this was that once gas was used by the Germans its use was seen as legitimate by the British and French; it was another down-spiral in an already seriously unlovely war.

Behind the regimental aid post was the advanced dressing station; behind that the casualty clearing station, behind that the base hospitals; and behind these the vast resources of the hospitals, nursing homes and converted country houses of Blighty. All these were linked by ambulances, both horse- and motor-powered, hospital trains, hospital barges and hospital ships, and run by that most important of military arms, the Royal Army Medical Corps. They might be the butt of soldierly jokes which interpreted RAMC as 'Run Away Mother's Coming' or 'Rob All My Comrades'; but these were the men whom the Tommy relied on to pull him through in time of trouble. At the time of a 'Big Push' their task was a heroic and a horrifying one, as they struggled to cope with a continuous tide of men with a vast and unpredictable range of wounds.

Private John Martin was an orderly at no. 9 General Hospital, Rouen, during the opening stages of the Battle of the Somme:

To begin with we had very little to do. We had got rid of every moveable patient and the wards were practically empty. Each ward held forty beds. Then early one morning the signal went for 'convoy' and for the next 72 hours the order of proceedings was: lift the stretchers from the ambulances, carry into the ward till it was full, go round washing face, hands and feet where these still existed, feed them, lift them on to stretchers and carry them out to ambulances unless the surgeon forbade further movement. Then the same again and again. Three times in the first twenty-four hours we filled the ward and emptied it, thrice in the second day and again during the third. In between times we had to do the regular work of feeding and washing those who remained in the ward who as time went on increased in number till there were no vacancies. There was also the occasional extra of carrying a stretcher to the operating theatre and back if he survived.

There were also the walking wounded who were examined and sent on without getting a chance to rest.

There was an incinerator in the hospital and I remember an old sweat who operated it recounting the incredible number of arms and legs he had disposed of in one day. I should estimate that during three days three hundred men went through our ward no. 20. There were nineteen other wards and a dozen other hospitals. Was it a nightmare? No, because we had no time to stop and think. We were too hard worked to feel at all. The only appropriate adjective was bloody and after it we were lousy as well from carrying discarded clothing to the incinerator.

There is perhaps a necessary postscript to this chapter. It has contained, inevitably, much harrowing material; but what is here printed was recorded by some of that handful of men who felt able to face up to the horrors with which they were confronted and write them down. For every one man that put pen — or pencil — to paper, there must have been hundreds if not thousands who wrote nothing, who simply indicated that they were 'in the pink' and resignedly carried on. And of those who wrote, how many would be prepared to speak of their experiences when they went home and mingled with people to whom the private world of the Western Front was entirely alien? The answer is, surely, very few. Their silence allowed people at home to retain their comfortable illusion that the trenches were, if dangerous, at least in some measure tolerable (an illusion that was in fact to produce a massive pendulum swing of emotion after the war when the reality was finally revealed) whereas in fact many of the khaki-clad figures whom they met in the streets of Blighty had lived through enough horrors to last them several lifetimes.

---

[1] I am grateful to Mr James Page of Belfast for sending me a copy of this letter and for providing me with the version printed above, in which gaps caused by the fading of the original pencil have been filled in and one or two remarkable (but irrelevant) spelling errors corrected.

Dear Rose…

'10 January 15
'Dear Rose, this is where we are at present where the cross is. Don't forget to answer and send me something nice with love from Sid xxx'

Sid Lewis, a private in the Army Service Corps, began sending postcards to his fiancée Rose from the moment he landed in Fance. His messages were always simple and cheerful. He was invariably in the best of health and concerned about the well-being of his family and friends back in Shepherd's Bush, London.

'11 April 15
'Dearest Rose, I am in the pink of condition regarding health, hoping you and all at home are the same. Yours ever, Sid xxx'

Now Sid and Rose are married.

'2 October 15
'Dearest I am in the pink & I hope you are alright safe & sound. Dearest I had no letter last night what have you forgot me. Cheer up my dear and be happy. I will be with you soon if all keeps as well as it is now . . . Lots of love & kisses from your loving husband for ever xxx'

148

'*6 August 16*
'*Dearest, have not received any letters today Monday. Still in the pink hoping you are feeling better. Don't forget to write freely and Rose I am broke. Darling one, this time two years ago we were happy, never mind roll on the finish. Cheery Oh lots of love & heaps of Kisses. yours for ever Sid xxx*
Cheery Oh.'

'*2 February 17*
'*Dearest I am still A1 don't send any letters to me yet but I will let you know when, Cheer Oh. Keep smiling. I will send you a letter tomorrow, yours for ever Sid xxx Lots of love & heaps of Kisses xx'*

Undated
'*Darling Rose, where you see the x is the place where we used to stand our cars and wait for orders. Really I wish I was with you. I am still yours for ever. Love & Kisses Sid xxx Save all these cards.'*

This was Sid Lewis's last card to his wife. A later hand has added the end of the story: 'Killed by gas. Age 23.'

14 'Take me back to dear old Blighty'

> I got a smack on my shoulder equipment and felt warm blood on my back. I went to the Dressing Station hoping I had got a wound that would put me in hospital in England. For that seemed the only hope of getting out of the war. We used to hope for a Blighty wound because we heard that the wounded were having a great time especially when convalescing. Taken everywhere, plenty good meals, etc. Therefore the only hope was a cushy flesh wound. Cushy meant easy and good.
>
> *Tom Macdonald, 9th Bn Royal Sussex Regt*

A 'Blighty wound', otherwise known as a 'Blighty one', or simply a 'Blighty', became for many men, particularly those who had somehow survived long months in the trenches, a kind of ultimate ambition — provided it was not too serious and in the right place. Tom Macdonald was not fortunate on this occasion: his wound was attended to and he was sent back to his war. When Corporal, formerly Private, George Morgan, 1st Bradford Pals, finally got the wound which he knew had been coming to him for months, he was fortunate; it was a perfect 'Blighty':

> It was August 1917. We were in front of Vimy and I had just received a parcel with a tin of strawberries in it. We had been at 'stand to' in the front line and we came down the communication trench to have some breakfast. I dug a little hole out of the trench to make a seat to sit on and we boiled some tea in our mess-tins. I had just opened the tin of strawberries and was going to eat them when a shell came over. I was sitting in my hole with my legs sticking out and there was a man going down the trench to the doctor's to have his eyes bathed (he had some trouble with his eyes) and this whizz-bang simply blew his head off — and a piece shrapnel hit me in the legs. As for that tin of strawberries I don't know where it went to.
>
> It was a wonderful 'Blighty'. I had often thought, where will I get hit? You can't go every day, month after month, just being missed. I didn't want it in my head — I didn't want to be barmy after the war — and used to think, I'd like it in my legs somewhere. And that was just where I got it. Everybody who saw it said 'What a lovely Blighty!' I went down to Rouen and then over to England, and everybody who came to dress my wound said 'What a lovely Blighty!' I think that was the best thing that ever happened to me.

George Morgan's wound was an honourable one, honourably obtained. There were less noble circumstances in which to earn that longed-for ticket home. Private Jack Sweeney wrote in a letter home in January 1917: 'My Captain has had to go into hospital, he was playing football and broke his knee, he thinks he is very lucky, so do we as it is a sure "Blighty one". No such luck for me.'

There were no absolutes in this matter; in a marginal case a ticket to Blighty might depend entirely on the whim of some doctor at the base. Indeed, there were doctors with a tendency to think of every soldier on sick parade who was not totally incapacitated as a malingerer for whom the only relevant treatment was another dose of life in the trenches. Lance-Sergeant Elmer Cotton met such a doctor at a Divisional Base Camp in 1915:

> He used to line the men up and go along the line asking each one, 'Well, and what's the matter with you my man?'
> 11 'Bad teeth, sir !'
> *answer* 'Well, I don't want you to eat the Germans.'
> (2) 'Consumption, sir!'
> *answer* 'Go up and spit at them.'
> (3) 'Short-sighted, sir!'
> *answer* 'How far can you see?'
> 'About 30 yards, sir.'
> *answer* 'The trenches are only 15 yds apart at some places. Up you go and the best of luck.'
> (4) 'Shot in the leg sir!'
> *answer* 'Up you go and shoot the man who shot you.'
> (5) 'Hit with shrapnel, sir!'
> *answer* 'Up you go and get your own back.'
> (6) 'Bad eyes, sir !'
> *answer* 'Just the man we want for listening posts.'
> The result of this particular doctor's methods was that one man with a varicose vein and another with his trigger finger shot off were returned to the firing line.

Harsh as this doctor plainly was, he might have had some justice on his side. Tommy was no saint and malingering by no means foreign to his nature. Tom Macdonald, convalescing at a Base Hospital after a gas attack, became aware that 'all kinds of rackets' were being tried by men eager to prolong their stay: 'My pal Johnny Bull had some soap pills he had made and reckoned if you swallowed them a little while before the Doctor saw you they would give you palpitations of the heart and he would not pass you fit.'

But there were other doctors who earned nothing but praise and admiration from their colleagues. Second Lieutenant Cyril Rawlins wrote home in a letter of August 1915:

> Our doc is a fine little Welshman who gave up a lucrative practice in Manchester to serve the country: he had a cellar full of patients last night and stood among the stretchers encouraging them and giving them cigarettes; see the eagerness with which the poor chaps reach out trembling hands for the

92 *'Blighty cases' whose condition no Tommies envied. Amputees showing the heroic cheerfulness expected of them in the presence of an official photographer, and also of the general public. (Q27815)*

'Woodbines' and the grateful sigh as they sink back inhaling the first few puffs. But some can't smoke: they lie very still, staring at the smoky ceiling, wide eyed. Heavy wounds, these . . . Two motor ambulances slide purring up to the entrance and the driver stumbles down the steps: 'Anything for us?' They take out the bad cases one by one, very tenderly: a shock-haired lad, not more than 19, heavily bandaged round the hand and arm, grins and looks down at the label printed on his blanket. 'Got my ticket for Blighty?' Right O.' Envious eyes follow the boy as he is loaded into the car.

Captain Lionel Ferguson, exhausted by lack of food and the strains of action, weakened by loss of blood and shocked at the sight of the dead and dying, collapsed in the dressing station at Albert and broke into tears (see Chapter 12). But after that the rituals of medical care took over and things began to go better. The first move was to Corbie, where the casualties were sorted. Ferguson was now destined for Blighty. He wrote subsequently in his diary:

> Left Corbie by motor for the railhead, at which was a big canvas hospital, near Amiens; but we did not leave here till evening, watching many trains of prisoners leave first. Arriving at Boulogne early next morning we were taken to

152

no. 14 General Hospital, having our wounds dressed and a good meal. I also managed to get some new underclothes, also a shave, a luxury I had not had for many days. We then rested till evening, getting called in time to be taken to the 'Blighty' ship . . . The joy of a hospital ship is great, for those who are able to enjoy it, and as I was, I did. We got everything we could wish for on the way over. We were met at the dock by many kind people who bestowed gifts upon us. The delights of being home once more gave us a smile which was hard to get rid of.

His good fortune held. He found himself within a matter of hours at Wilton House, near Salisbury, a superb country house which the Countess of Pembroke had converted into a private hospital:

It was late evening when we arrived, but Lady P was most kind, coming herself to see to our comfort. We were given an excellent dinner, after which we were put to bed for 48 hours, whilst our clothes got fumigated. Eight officers were in our ward, in a beautiful room on the ground floor.

Ecstatic welcomes to the heroic wounded were standard, particularly at the time of the great battles. Some men could not stomach these ritualistic returns home, which seemed simply to emphasize the gulf of incomprehension which divided the soldier and the civilian.

At Waterloo I was with the first party of wounded out of the train and they put us in private cars. There was the fatheaded crowd, just as you read about it, gaping and throwing cigarettes etc., and the whole ride was most detestable through the heart of London, with me perched up in front, not quite in such a bad state as on reaching Rouen, but nevertheless with two days dirt and beard, hatless and dishevelled, and a dangling sleeve.

Lance-Corporal Roland Mountfort, 10th Bn Royal Fusiliers

Arriving home, covered in blood and mud, we were met by cheering crowds at Charing Cross Station. But we were in no mood to be entertained and were glad to get to hospital.

Lieutenant H. C. Lovely, 2nd Bn Bedfordshire Regt

All these men were to survive their wounds and the war, but there were many thousands for whom a 'Blighty' wound was not just a temporary relief from the trenches; for whom in fact it was the end of all prospects of a normal life; who might be doomed to long years in ex-servicemen's homes or hospitals; who would become the inevitable wrecks of a large-scale modern war — heroic and pitiable to begin with, later to be largely forgotten.

There was a less painful way of getting to 'dear old Blighty', even if it ensured only the briefest and most tantalizing of visits: leave.

93   *Men about to go on leave showing their leave passes to the photographer at Poperinghe,
railhead to the Ypres Salient, 30 September 1917. (Q3096)*

One evening I was told my officer had been to see me about going home on
leave. Oh, what a feeling! No one but the Tommy knows what it is. After ten
months of war and all its horrors, I was getting leave to go home, to dear old
England, or rather, to call it by our favourite name, 'Blighty' for seven clear
days.

Corporal F.W. Billman 9th Bn East Surrey Regt

There was an unavoidable consequence of being informed that you were due to go on
leave: suddenly you seemed to be especially vulnerable and the trenches especially
dangerous.

On Tuesday I hear that I am for leave on the following Saturday. How well I
remember the next two days. The old Fritz seemed to be after me everywhere
and I certainly was more times in the fire trench than I need have been just to
prove to myself that I wasn't nervy but oh my! How I longed for Friday when
I would leave the trenches. Nothing else mattered.

Captain J.H. Mahon, 8th Bn King's Liverpool Regt

94 *Soldiers dispersing after the arrival of the leave train from Folkestone at Victoria Station, London. (Q30508)*

The normal pattern for the journey home was a long walk to a railhead, a long wait for a military train and hours of kicking heels in Boulogne (or Le Havre) before being allowed on the boat for England. Captain Harry Yoxall and two fellow officers, going on leave in March 1917, attempted to add a few hours to their all-too-brief taste of home by aiming for the afternoon packet from Boulogne instead of the evening boat by which they would normally have sailed. When they reached Hazebrouck en route for the coast they did not wait for the military train but climbed on board the first civilian one:

> There followed an agonizing journey, in which the train crawled round and about Northern France at a pace amazingly slow and with halts every quarter of an hour: but eventually dumped our anguish-torn souls at Boulogne at 2.10 p.m. and after a frenzied rush to the docks we found that the boat — did not leave till 4 p.m.!!
>
> So we lunched in comfort, had a shave, went down to the docks again, slipped aboard when the press was at its greatest and with our tickets unexamined: and hay-ho! For England, home and beauty.

To set foot in Blighty after all those months of war was an overwhelming experience. Sergeant Albert George, 120th Battery, Royal Field Artillery, landed in Southampton on

1 December 1915 after 'sixteen months forced absence': 'Directly we landed we jumped into a waiting train which took us to Waterloo and I am sure we were the Happiest men in England although our Happiness we knew was short-liv'd.'

Corporal Billman, who unlike Captain Yoxall and friends took the evening sailing from Boulogne, found himself in London at 12.30 a.m. on a Sunday morning, with a night and the best part of a day to kill before he could make for home. He felt conspicuously different from the crowds strolling the Sunday streets:

> You can imagine how dirty I felt among all the people wearing their Sunday best, but that did not trouble me, as it was not my fault, and it showed that I had been doing my little bit for my king and country. Still, I had another journey to do, and this time it was to Norfolk, and to the best place on earth — home.
>
> I arrived there at about 8 p.m., meeting my mother on the way as she was just taking a quiet stroll, and since I had not been able to let anyone know I was coming what a surprise it was for her! It was not long before I was sitting down for a good meal, and the kettle was singing, just the same as it used to do before this awful war commenced.

The soldier on leave was always a man apart; even in the later phases of the war, when the energies of Britain's young womenfolk were added to those of her young men in the great drive towards victory, he was still not without honour. Driver R.L. Venables, Royal Field Artillery, went home in September 1918:

> The train from London terminated at Rotherham, and from there I went by tram to Mexborough; the tram was packed with women, many of them standing and they were evidently returning home from some kind of men's work for their clothes, hands and faces were very dirty. As soon as I had pushed my way on to the tram, one of the seated women got up and told me, in a resolute manner, to sit down and I refused, whereupon all the other women called out 'sit down lad', so reluctantly I had to comply, not being keen on having a scrap with a lot of women.

But as those precious days of leave began, all too frequently a jarring note was struck.

> Was I glad to be back in the bosom of my family? But one thing that annoyed me very much was to be met by the 'old uns' who usually said to me, 'What, home again? When are you going back?' We'd had quite enough of it without going back.

So wrote Private Thomas Bickerton, 11th Battalion Royal Sussex Regiment. Tom Macdonald, a fellow member of his regiment, recorded the same experience, with one other standard and equally insensitive question:

When I walked the old streets and met old friends, the first thing they would say was 'When are you going back?' and 'Do you like it over there?' They had no idea of the conditions and it was stupid to try and explain.

The two worlds — those of the soldier and of the people at home — were too far apart and the gap was unbridgeable. Civilians, fed by the heroic propaganda of the newspapers, perhaps even confirmed in their misconceptions by the natural restraint shown by many if not most soldiers in their letters home, had little idea of the effect of their clumsy but quite natural curiosity on men who for a very brief while were trying to forget the awfulness of the environment from which they had been temporarily released. Not that there was much chance of forgetting; the reality of the Western Front was only a few days behind them and only a few days away.

London seemed as familiar as ever; I might never have left it; but at the back of my mind, whether I was sitting in a music hall or having dinner with friends, there was a vision always present — the contrast between that front line and the happy theatre.

Major R.S. Cockburn, 10th King's Royal Rifle Corps

Lance-Corporal Roland Mountfort, 10th Battalion Royal Fusiliers, also found that he could not escape from his constant awareness of 'that front line' and that this made him bad company. Back in France he wrote to his mother in apology:

I am afraid you must have found my society a trifle dull. I realized at the time that I wasn't being exactly brilliant, but didn't seem to be able to help it. I think it was due in a large measure to the subconscious oppression of the knowledge of my imminent return to Army life, which after two years I still loathe with all the hatred of which I am capable. We must have another holiday after the war, when the horizon is all clear.

Then, all too soon, it was over: time to go back.

Those seven days passed quicker than any I have known. Oh those Good-Byes and that bone in throat feeling.

Private Tom Macdonald, 9th Bn Royal Sussex Regt

I shall never forget the parting from my wife and kiddies, it was cruel. But I would go through the same again for another leave, for we spent a very happy time altogether.

Lance-Corporal James Gingell, Royal Engineers

Sergeant Albert George, who had thought himself and his comrades the 'happiest men in England' just a few days before, was now very much subdued. He wrote in his diary:

Last walk round town, decide to catch the 12.25 up. Break down while saying Good Bye to Mr and Mrs Daniells — decide to go by earlier train — leave without saying Good Bye to Daisy and Annie — very childish of me. Go to station with S. — catch 11.40 up — very sorry having to leave dear old Watford — miserable ride to London. Very pitiful sight at Waterloo — many men and women crying — Bagpipes playing 'Keep the Home Fires Burning' etc. Enter train 3.45 p.m. thinking of the girl I was leaving behind and wondering if I should ever see her again! Train starts 4.0 p.m. — inwardly very down-hearted — Good Bye London — Wish the Kaiser were dead and peace restored.

Then, once again, the soldier was on the boat bound for France — but going back from leave was worlds away from going to France for the first time.

I remember on the after deck of the boat were troops returning off leave: they were mostly very quiet and deep in thought; and on the foredeck were men of a new draft going over for the first time. They were singing the latest songs and laughing and joking — they did not know what they were in for.

Private Tom Macdonald, 9th Bn Royal Sussex Regt

For some, however, it was preferable to be in France than in Britain. Home sapped the vitality, muddied the certainties, and the incomprehension of the civilian made one a stranger.

So my leave has gone: and I go back to the war for the third time. It was not so hard as I had expected. England is clearly no place to be in now: civilian opinion is disquieted and peevish: and I find there once more all the doubts of personal conduct and general policy, so it is good to escape from that atmosphere to one where one sees clearly and one's way lies straight ahead.

So wrote Captain Harry Yoxall, who had been so keen to add to his time at home by catching the early boat from Boulogne. It was not the first time he had expressed such sentiments. At the end of an earlier leave he had written: 'Good as leave was, I have quite enjoyed getting back.'

But leave could be an embittering experience, returning a man to the trenches unhappy, frustrated and deprived. Sometimes the pages of a diary tell a tragic story: of a young man of intense vitality desperate to taste the pleasures of life before the opportunity is snatched from him and whose inability to find what he is looking for wrings from him a cry of protest. Such a diary is that of Second Lieutenant Kenneth Macardle, the brave young officer par excellence of the 17th Manchesters. He was just 26 when he spent what was to be his last leave in Blighty. Back with his battalion on the Somme, only a few weeks before his death, he wrote in his diary that he had 'seen a lot of people and a lot of plays and ate a lot of food and had a lot of baths — and on the day I left I had a long, delicious but solitary lunch at the Piccadilly.' But one element was missing.

To thoroughly enjoy leave one should be engaged, or married (very newly married), or have — well — a friend with a delicate but overriding love of sensation. Failing this one has a rebelliousness; places one always loved seem intolerably dull; people one has found thrilling ere now fill one with dissatisfaction. Busy days have fallen flat. The ordinary dinner at the Carlton, box at the Gaiety, supper at Ciro's programme is tiresome and dull — it is hard indeed to keep up the illusion of enjoyment; one says 'Well good night, see you tomorrow' with a dreary feeling of stalemate and a sense of acting indifferently done. One enters the lift at one's hotel in a villainously bad humour.

There are only nine days of leave after a hundred of war. A hundred of discomfort and hard work, plain necessary work, stupid necessary work. A hundred days and nights of uneventful dullness and of wearing strain; a hundred days and nights of 'keeping cheerful' — of pretending you don't mind dirt and discomfort and are quite used to being killed: — and then nine days and nights of leave. Surely they should be more than a holiday full of comfort and pleasure. One needs days of lazy dalliance and luxurious spending; eyes sleepy from adoring someone with a low laugh and inexplicable sunlight in her hair — someone with soft clothes; leading up to nights of madness — nights drunk with loveliness and love.

But I must take a fatigue to clean trenches at Maricourt and it is a very wet night and the roads are very muddy; and first I must have my dinner on the door covered with newspaper and laid from a windowsill to a packing case, and sit on the carpenter's bench which it was such a stroke of luck to find and which makes the mess so perfectly top-hole!

Cheer O! it's a jolly old war.

15 'Cheer O! it's a jolly old war'

'Cheer O! it's a jolly old war.' It is a significant and revealing sentence. It has a hint of world-weariness, of shoulder-shrugging resignation, but there is no defeatism and the generally accepted determination to slog on and see things through is quietly understood. It suggests a mug of scotch (or a mess-tin of tea) raised in a dugout on a wet night in not-so-cushy trenches in the middle or later years of the war. This is not the naive crusading mood of 1914. The Army in France — a far cry from the tiny expeditionary force that had marched towards its first rendezvous with the enemy at Mons — had become a vast and many-sided organism, a self-contained society, with its own rituals, its special disciplines, its own codes. Soldiering on the Western Front was no longer a simple matter of firing guns and 'biffing the Boche'. It singled out successes and failures, made heroes of the strong, submitted the personalities of weaker men to often unbearable pressures, produced animosities between one group and another, created privileges for some which led to countervailing resentments in others, shook many men's beliefs to their foundations. Old assumptions and received attitudes were all thrown into the melting pot. There were new challenges and new temptations. What follows are not complete statements about these less discussed but important aspects of this now hugely complicated conflict; merely a few episodes, a few fragments of experience, a few comments and descriptions have been brought together, to raise a few issues, air a few grievances, clarify a few attitudes.

Morale — and Leave

In 1916 Sapper Garfield Powell, Royal Engineers, wrote in his diary:

> As an army we are darned badly treated. Officers claim to get leave every three months and get it. Battalion and Company Sgt-Majors claim leave every four months and again get it (being called Sir by their inferiors in rank not being sufficient sop to their self-love). In what army (barring the national armies of Germany or Russia) would such a system be in vogue? The officers in most regiments take very little more risk than their privates. Their bodies are not fatigued by constant and hard work and they are no more useful to the Army than privates. Why should the fools in higher command allow it? Why should 'gentlemen' take it as nothing less than their due? Ay, what fools we all are!

This is an eloquent outburst, all the more meaningful in that the writer was a university graduate with a B.Sc. in Chemistry and Mathematics who would almost certainly have been a candidate for a commission but for the social accident that he was a miner's son. Certainly in this case he is an intelligent commentator — no sheep accepting without compunction the patently unfair dispensations of his superiors. Everybody knew that ordinary soldiers might go well over the year without leave, even as much as 18 months, while his officers seemed by contrast to be always making for Blighty. Some might accept that in this as in so many aspects of life at the front the officer did far better than the soldier. But for many this disparity in the highly personal matter of home leave became a real and growing grievance. This was privilege not on the military but the human level. It meant deprivation not only for the Tommy himself but also for his parents, wife, sweetheart, children; and this was an area where all men were, or at any rate thought they should be, equal.

Captain J.H. Dible, RAMC, wrote in his commonplace book in September 1917 that 'a very definite and serious current of discontent and dissatisfaction has indubitably come into existence'. He added that he was convinced that it was 'the question of leave which is at the root of the larger part of the discontent around us'. The entry continues:

> The facts of the case at present, as for the last two years, are these. An ordinary officer gets leave, on an average, once in every six or seven months: the man gets his on an average of once in fifteen to nineteen months. This is a perfectly inexcusable state of affairs and should not be allowed to continue for a minute. In the British army the officer, on campaign, is supposed to share the hardships of his men. Here there is a gross disparity between the treatment of the two.

(It should be added that no attempt has been made to reconcile these figures with Sapper Garfield Powell's; disparity in the matter of leave was such that I have no doubt both statements were true within the experience of the men concerned.)

The autumn of 1917 produced such a serious situation that questions were asked about the subject in Parliament and, Dible noted, circulars were sent round urging that 'every effort should be made to give leave to men who had not had it for twelve months or more'. In October Captain Lionel Ferguson was noting in his diary: 'We are trying to send on leave the men long overdue: men left my company today who have not been home for 20 months.'

Dible had one more inequality to record in his book: the almost inevitable fact that the Staff

> from the people who frame the leave regulations to the latest learner in the headquarters office who signs the leave tickets get their leave regularly every three or four months. The officer himself, well treated as he is by comparison with the men, has his own grievances in the superior treatment allotted to the Staff. He sees that they go on leave twice to his one, that the way is paved for them by special trains; that boats are reserved for their use by which he is not allowed to travel. On his return from leave the ordinary officer has to catch a

train leaving Victoria at 6.50 a.m.: the gilded Staff travel down in comfort after their breakfast on a train which leaves London at 10.30 or thereabouts.

The soldier in the Middle East or Salonika would of course have one general comment on all who served on the Western Front, whether 'gilded Staff', officer or man: that they were lucky to have any home leave at all.

Discipline

In 1916 Private F.H. Bastable, 7th Battalion Royal West Kent Regiment, came out of a hard spell in the trenches and went into billets behind the line. The next morning, being mess orderly, he did not have time to clean and unload his rifle:

> When on parade for rifle inspection, after opening the bolts and closing them again the second time as it did not suit the officer the first time, I accidentally let off a round. I had to go before the CO and got No. 1 Field Punishment. I was tied up against a wagon by ankles and wrists for two hours a day, 1 hour in the morning and 1 in the afternoon in the middle of winter and under shellfire.
>
> There were two wagons with one soldier on each wheel. It was in what had been a French school, and I could hear the shells going overhead and was frightened one might land near as it was battalion headquarters. If one had we could not have got away or ducked down. But the worst part was the cold. After we were untied, the guard room sergeant who was walking up and down made us run round the playground to get us warm again. The Colonel who passed sentence said he had to as an example to the rest of the battalion.

Private Archie Surfleet witnessed a man undergoing Field Punishment No. 1 on the Somme front in July 1916 and found the sight horrifying:

> A lot of guns were lined up very regimentally and a number of limbers, spotlessly polished, stood beside them. At first, I could not believe my eyes, but as we came quite close to the guns, I saw that one of the artillerymen was lashed with rope to the wheel of one of the limbers. He was stretched out, cruciform-fashion, his arms and legs wide apart, secured to the wheel. His head lolled forward as he shook it to drive away the flies. I don't think I have ever seen anything which so disgusted me in my life and I know the feelings amongst our boys was very near to mutiny at such inhuman punishment. I have seen some Infantry lads lashed to trees at Warnimont Woods, sometimes as many as five or six, spaced out amongst the trees looking like so many American Indian prisoners about to be scalped and that seemed an anti-British sort of way to punish a man for any fault, but the expression on the face of this half-crucified gunner got us all groggy. I have never heard such expressions of disgust from the troops before. I'd like to see the devils who devised this having

an hour or two lashed up like that. The milder, No. 2 Field Punishment consists of full pack-drill; not ordinary drilling, but with a police-sergeant standing by, shouting 'Right turn, left turn, about turn . . .' one after the other, all done at something near the 'double'. It seems hellish that anyone should be treated like this and I am sure it cannot make them any better soldiers. I suppose troops on active service have to be dealt with severely, but these degrading punishments are only creating a feeling of utter disgust amongst the others; I am quite sure the corrective effect on the individual is more than negatived by its influence on his pals.

Field Punishment No.1 was abandoned later in the war but military discipline never lost its harsh quality. Death by firing squad, as has already been mentioned was not uncommon. In addition to the 332 cases of death sentences carried out, many men were condemned to death and later reprieved; it no doubt being part of the military psychology to assume that there could be no better incentive to a wrongdoer to improve his ways than the threat of being deprived of the opportunity to do so. Private Henry Bolton, 1st Battalion East Surrey Regiment, recorded in his diary how on 1 July 1915 he and his comrades

> were formed up to listen to 4 Court Martials of our own Regt they were all for sleeping at their post, the first to be read out was that of L/Cpl Wilson one of my old boys of Devonport, his crime was not serious as he was in support at the time when caught. The others were serious as they were on sentry in the firing line and they were sentenced to death but the sentence was not carried out, the good work of the Regt saving them.

An incident that particularly shocked the Bradford Pals was the execution of two members of the 2nd Pals (18th Battalion West Yorkshire Regiment) shortly before the disaster of 1 July 1916. Private George Morgan:

> These two men got drunk and they wandered away and got caught and were brought back and were charged with absenteeism on active service. If it had been in England they would have got seven days CB. They laughed it off, they thought wandering away was just something or nothing; but they were court-martialled and they were sentenced to be shot, subject to Sir Douglas Haig. He could have said no, but he didn't. So they were shot. They were described as being killed in action. Of course it was kept fairly dark, but their family got to know about it. I remember a letter years ago in the local paper, in which some lady was asking 'what happened to my brother?' That was what had happened to her brother.

To this story Morgan added this footnote: 'They didn't shoot any Australians. They would have rioted. They weren't like us. We were docile.'

Sex

Private Archie Surfleet, 13th Battalion East Yorkshire Regiment, much quoted in this book, kept a diary during 1916–18, wrote it up in the 1920s and expanded and edited it 40 years later. In a Preface to his final version he wrote:

> A lot of excellent books, films, plays and television productions have covered many aspects of life in the Great War . . . There has been a lot of talk of blood and horror and devastation; some of it is true. Other accounts, written by much abler (and braver) authors, have given so much prominence to sex, there seems a danger that 'our war' may only be remembered as a series of drunken orgies interspersed with a few cases of rape and almost nightly immoral relations with every available French and Belgian female. This sort of picture is far from the truth. At times it was bloody and terrifying but, as for sex, most of the females were too old or too tired doing a man's job to be interested. There were 'Red Lamps' (brothels) in some of the bigger towns but they were, comparatively, little used. The propaganda against VD before we went out and later was good enough to deter the vast majority of overseas soldiers and those who 'caught a dose' suffered so much in so many ways their misery killed the 'urge' and discretion usually triumphed. I never saw any girl molested in any way; they were mostly treated with the utmost respect by the troops.

This is a comprehensive and important statement and perhaps goes a long way to explain why sex is a subject rarely touched on, even obliquely, in the diaries and letters of the time or in the later reminiscences of old soldiers when they might perhaps have been expected to divulge more, say, than in letters likely at some stage to catch the censor's eye. The Western Front was inevitably a masculine and very public world. The sight of a female was a rarity and opportunities for any sexual relationship other than a commercial one were rarer still. Women were remote, occupants of a far-off idealized horizon. One young subaltern watched avidly at a station up the line as two young 'female guardians of a coffee urn' dispensed their sustenance to tired Tommies: 'For months to come we are going to a land peopled with one sex. Do they realize how much they stand for in our eyes?' (Lieutenant V. F. Eberle, Royal Engineers, 48th Division). In the same way a pretty young nurse at a base hospital would seem like a visitant from another planet; but unless you were an RAMC man you were only likely to see a vision at a time when you were incapable of doing anything other than dumbly admire.

Of course there were exceptions to Archie Surfleet's generalization about the unavailability of the young and attractive among the French or Belgian women whom the soldier met when out from the line. But all too frequently the customs of the French peasantry were too strict to allow of easy dalliance.

> There was a girl about 17 years old, I fell for her, her name was Madolien Vatblag. We could never get alone together, because the mother would always turn up. But love finds a way, in the evening we used to sit at the table with a

book on French and English and I would point to sentences and she would read and point to answers and our hands would clasp under the table and we would press our knees together. It was frustrating, I could never get a moment alone with her (perhaps it's just as well). We corresponded years after. I had to send her letters to a friend in London to be translated.

But Tom Macdonald, whose story this is, goes on to emphasize the rarity of cases even as innocuous as this. 'Many thought we had plenty of mademoiselles but at times months passed without a sight of civilian girls, especially on the Somme. And when we did get to a village where they were, there was too much competition.'

There were, of course, as Surfleet indicates in the statement at the head of this section, brothels; such institutions have always sprung into existence in the presence of great armies and in the context of the Western Front they were inevitable.

One afternoon, whilst in camp, two or three of us decided, out of curiosity, to see what it was like, and with no intention of making the usual use of the amenities, to visit No. 1 'Red Lamp' Establishment. This was one of the French Government licensed brothels.

We had been given to understand that, at such places, there was a bar, where one might sit and order drinks, like in an ordinary estaminet, without going any further. This place was a large house, with '1' painted on the door. In we went and took our places at a table in the bar. 'Madame' appeared, and we ordered drinks, but she intimated that they were not allowed to serve drinks until after 6 p.m., but said we could 'go upstairs' now!

We said 'No', and that we wanted drinks first, but Madame was adamant, and rang a bell. In trooped five or six girls, all most scantily dressed! I have never seen such an unattractive collection of females in my life! Not one was in the least pretty though all were quite young. Some were downright ugly! I should have thought that it was enough to put anyone off completely, even if he had gone in with the usual intention!

Madame, and the girls too, all began saying that we should 'go upstairs' but we said 'No', and that we would come back after six that evening (having really no such intention), have drinks, and then 'go upstairs' after which we hurriedly left, to a torrent of abuse, in both French and English.

We were glad to get outside! At least I had added to my French vocabulary! In spite of the unattractive appearance of the merchandise, this establishment obviously did a good trade. We often used to watch ASC lorries drive up, stop, the driver disappear inside, and, in an incredibly short time reappear and drive off! This always intrigued us! 'Rapid Fire' with a vengeance!

Rifleman H.G.R. Williams, London Rifle Brigade

Brothels inevitably meant that there was the danger of venereal disease. That danger implied the necessity of VD inspections. Here is Private Surfleet again, describing such an inspection in 1917:

Yesterday we all lined up before the Medical Officer for what the troops call a 'short-arm inspection'. It could only have been for one purpose which, four years ago, would have made a young man flush with shame. But, today, it does not seem degrading and I must confess as we lined up facing each other with only our shirts on, the thought flashed through my mind that it was better for us all to show, however crudely, the absence or presence of that horrible disease the Doc. was looking for. That shows how much we have changed and God only knows how much more we shall change before the end of this blasted lot.

One other subject is worth touching on in this section, even though it is worlds away from 'Red Lamps' and venereal disease. The writer is that idealistic young officer, Second Lieutenant Cyril Rawlins, and his theme is the paramount importance of marriage at a time when the flower of the nation's youth was subject to the possibility of death or injury on a massive scale:

I consider it the duty of every fit man to get married, whether he is at home, or a soldier only home on five days leave. The 'marry after the war' idea is very nice, but then the blunt fact is that for many there will be no 'after the war'. Our best and finest men are daily being killed and wounded, all our best blood going to waste and our race is bound to suffer terrible depreciation in consequence and we ought to do all in our power to lessen this for the sake of the country's future. If the best happens, every single man will have to marry 'after the war': if the worst happens, don't you think it is better for a man to leave behind a young widow and a robust child, duly provided for by Government, than an unmarried fiancée, who, moreover, will never have the chance of marrying? In my mind there is no doubt of this: it is cold sense.

Medals

After heavy fighting on 11 April 1917 in the vicinity of the new Hindenburg line ('The Lincs went like bulls for it') Private Jack Sweeney wrote home:

There were over 100 men recommended in the last battle including myself, 40 of them are dead and I think that there are too many for all of us to get a medal. I suppose that the dead men will get one at least their parents will, they deserve one more than all of us that are alive . . . All the boys deserved a medal as I am sure they all did as much as one another but those that were recommended were seen by the officers to do these things.

There was a reasonably generous distribution of medals and honours in the war: over 31,000 Military Crosses for officers, over 110,000 Military Medals for NCOs and men. In addition and more rarely there were Distinguished Conduct Medals for NCOs and men and Distinguished Service Orders for officers — and, an honour out on its own, the

95   *Presentation of medals, to soldiers of the 56th Infantry Brigade. The standard assumption was that, while many medals were awarded for genuine gallantry, many others 'came up with the rations'. (Q239)*

Victoria Cross, which could be won by any officer or man for bravery of a particularly outstanding kind. Over 500 were won in France and Belgium.

The problem with the distribution of honours was that it was, as Sweeney's letter implies, distinctly arbitrary. Often the most courageous acts went unrewarded simply because they were not seen by an officer. As George Morgan commented: 'We couldn't be recommended for bravery for July 1st 1916 because there were no officers left. There was no one to recommend us, only ourselves.'

The other major source of grievance was that those who were well clear of danger seemed to fare substantially better in the matter of awards than those who were doing the fighting. George Morgan again:

> A friend of mine could type — he used to work in Bradford Town Hall and he got a job down at Divisional Headquarters. I met him one day and he said: 'George, I've been mentioned in despatches!' So I said, 'You what?' 'I've been mentioned in despatches,' he said. I said, 'What the hell for? You never saw a trench!' I was staggered: he had never been further than a typewriter 30 or 40 miles away from the trenches. Medals were ten a penny down at the base. A chap got the DCM for baking bread down at Étaples. You could get a DCM for washing the general's dog!
>
> I had another friend, Sergeant Joe Calvert, who was awarded the French

Médaille Militaire. I said, 'What have you done for it?' He said, 'I don't know, no more than anybody else.' Joe went on leave and afterwards a copy of the local paper was sent out to the trenches to a neighbour of his, a friend of mine called Whitworth. And there it was in the paper: 'WAR HERO COMES HOME ON LEAVE . . . The modest hero refused to disclose how he had won the coveted honour . . .' And my friend Whitworth was reading this out of the local paper and he was rolling laughing, because, of course, Joe *didn't know!*

Undoubtedly, countless medals were genuinely won and in the location where they were meant to be won, in the centre of the storm. Captain Harry Yoxall was recommended for a Military Cross after the fighting on the Somme in September 1916 ('I did some fairly useful work getting the bombs up: on one occasion too I got back three wounded and a German machine gun'). He registered quiet pleasure in his diary when the news that the recommendation had been accepted came through:

I am now officially Captain H.W. Yoxall, MC. This I learnt from Col Potter over the phone after dinner. And very nice too. I'm very glad, principally for the people's sake. But it's a very lucky one. How many better deeds went unrecorded and unrewarded that day it is impossible to say.

In March 1917 he went to receive his medal from the hands of the King himself.

This morning I attended the investiture at the Palace. It was a very dull show; we are kept waiting a long while in a very stuffy atmosphere and then filed up like a lot of schoolboys for prizes. The King, with wonderful originality, asked me which battalion I belonged to and he shook me by the hand.

In February 1918 Second Lieutenant E.J. Ruffell, 342 Siege Battery, Royal Garrison Artillery, found himself (in a flurry of 'spit and polish and speculation as to who was to be honoured') at a ceremony at which certain Belgian awards were to be made to various deserving British officers. The occasion, albeit held in a muddy field, was lavishly adorned by 'mighty ones'. Among those present were 'the 2nd Army General and our own general and a Belgian General representing the King of the Belgians, with trailing behind them Brigade Majors, Staff Captains and Red tabbed subs with blue eyes and no ambition'. It was going to be an occasion of some embarrassment; the whole of Ruffell's Brigade was there. 'The RSM "broke" the flag at the masthead. The Colonel hoarsely "shunned" the Brigade. The Brigade then presented "aps" without any casualties and "serloped aps" [i.e. presented arms and sloped arms] again with a sob of relief.'
Then one by one those to be honoured were called forth:

'2 Lieut E. J. Ruffell, 342 Battery' — 'Chevalier de l'Ordre de la Couronne' with palm and 'Croix de Guerre'. Blushing and feeling a silly idiot I jerked myself forward, saluted, had the ironmongery pinned on my stomach, shook hands with all the Generals, saluted, 'about turned', nearly fell over my feet and wobbled back. A half cheer — quickly suppressed from my battery. And then on top of that, we the Decorated ones had to stand alongside the Brass hats while the Brigade marched past giving us 'eyes right' — never felt such a fool in my life. I felt so sorry for the poor chaps — as they marched by with their heads and necks in a permanent crick. It was a particularly muddy piece of ground and they couldn't tell where their feet were going. I felt as if I had lost a shilling and found sixpence! Because I knew that several of our men whilst with the Belgian Army had been recommended for a Decoration for bravery, and it seemed to me so unfair that only I, because I was an officer, had got anything.

However, I am pleased to say that later in the Official Gazette when my name appeared, the following June, their names appeared as well for the 'Croix de Guerre', but unfortunately by that time we had lost about half the men recommended by wounds or sickness.

However, most men's attitude to medals would have coincided with that of Private Sweeney, who, having told his wife that he had been recommended for an award (which he felt, rightly as it turned out, that he would not get), added: 'Blow the medals, as long as I live to scrape out of this war I shall be satisfied with a tin medal.'

Front Line versus Staff

When in November 1916 Second Lieutenant Norman Collins, 1/6th Battalion Seaforth Highlanders, completed his work as burial officer (see Chapter 13), he collected the paybooks of the men he had buried in sandbags and delivered them to Brigade Headquarters. He wrote in a letter home:

> Brigade H.Q. amazed me. It was in a deep dugout in the chalk with electric light, officers very immaculate, parcels from Fortnum and Mason. The contrast with the front line and No Man's Land shocked me.

Captain Harry Yoxall, a month after being involved in the hard fighting on the Somme for which he won his MC, found himself for a day or two 'living in luxury in a chateau'. It was a billet like no other. He commented:

> One can understand that those people at Army and Corps headquarters behind the line some thirty miles, with nice châteaus in which to live, are in no hurry to end the war. It was nice to sleep in Mme la Contesse's room and dress in her boudoir — though one felt it was rather an intrusion.

However, his spell of staff work was not the easy ride that most men in the front line thought it to be: 'You know the old jest — Question "If bread is the staff of life what is the life of the Staff?" Answer "One long loaf." Well, it isn't true. I've never been so busy in my life.'

*96   Staff officers at Hazebrouck:
a sight highly displeasing to
Sergeant Cotton.
(E (AUS) 1092)*

Nevertheless the reputation of the staff was unredeemable. Captain J.H. Dible, RAMC, expressed the standard viewpoint when he wrote of staff officers 'who are all too frequently nincompoops who think to hide their vacuity behind an eye glass'. And Major R.S. Cockburn was moved almost to a litany of protest when out 'on rest' in June 1917:

> I get one football field at St Hilaire, but it is very small.
>
> There seems to be no help forthcoming in anything from the Staff. They tell us to play football and put us where there is no ground to play on. They actually order sets of cricket things but there is nowhere to play.
>
> They tell us to bathe, and there is nowhere to bathe.
>
> They tell us we shall be in very comfortable billets and several officers have no beds: three sleep in one tent.
>
> They give us no material to improve the billets and make beds with, when we ask for it.
>
> They are miserably inefficient.

(It is fair to add that in checking and revising his account of the war Major Cockburn deleted the final sentence.)

The odium against those who had a permanently 'cushy' war rose to such a point that in March 1918, Captain Arthur Gibbs, 1st Battalion Welsh Guards, could write home:

I wonder if you have heard of the list of Stormtruppers which I am told is going the round of the club in London now. To be a member of the Stormtruppers it is essential to have been in the army since the beginning of the war, and never to have been in the trenches with one's regiment, in other words to have a real soft job for the whole of the war. It caused no ordinary flutter, I believe.

One particular grievance was that the 'high-ups' never put themselves in any danger of being hurt. Captain Yoxall noted, not without dry amusement, the visit of General S.T. Lawford, 41st Divisional Commander, known to his men as 'Sydney', to the proximity of the front line:

Sydney went round the trenches, I hear they chased him up a communicagger-tragger [communication trench] with whizz-bangs and oil jars [mortar shells] and that he didn't stay to investigate where they were coming from. But after all you don't want a first chop divisional commander taken off by a miserable Minnie [*Minenwerfer*]; it's not his job.

Perhaps for a final comment one might turn to that remarkable reporter of Western Front conditions, Lance-Sergeant Elmer Cotton, of the 5th Northumberland Fusiliers:

To see some of the officers of our army lounging about and 'swanking' in somebody else's motor car, and in such large numbers at Hazebrouck and such like towns well behind the line, would disgust the average and energetic business man.

Why doesn't God stop the War?

Plainly this question worried the mother of Lieutenant Cyril Rawlins, as it worried many people at the time. In his letter of 1 July 1915 he wrote:

Dear Little Mother,
I too have wondered why God should allow such a catastrophe as the war: we cannot guess at the purpose, and as you say it is taking all our, *everyone's* best men. We are fighting for the right, and more than this, we are fighting for our very life as an Empire and as a nation against a foe without mercy, and whatever happens, whatever sacrifice we have to make we *must* beat him. This we have always before us. *The enemy must not take Calais!* If they could, our Empire built up for us by centuries of toil and sacrifice, our nation, would cease to exist, we should be lost as surely as if England sank beneath the sea. You in England cannot realize this as we do who live as it were shoring up a dike, holding back the pitiless sea of brutality and slaughter.

For Rawlins there was no doubt: God was on England's side. In an earlier letter to his mother he had written: 'Another day: the 312th day of the war! Three hundred and twelve dawns since this horror came upon the world . . . Thank God a new day dawns in my fair green England undefiled.'

Private Archie Surfleet, however, sensed an insoluble problem in the fact that the enemy was claiming divine support at the same time:

> Saw some fellows with a German helmet, quite a massive affair with a spread-eagle and a scroll saying *'Mitt Gott für Koenig und Faterland'*. Strikes me God must think we are a pack of fools: surely he can't be on both sides. What a christian world this must be.

What about the Tommy? What did Christianity mean to him in this world of deliberate slaughter? Archie Surfleet's diary has this to say: 'Not many of us are religious in the true sense of the word though a lot of us turn to God for help and comfort when we are afraid: that does not make us religious.' But he added: 'One thing does strike me as significant: there have been several confirmations out here in France.' He also had nothing but praise for the chaplains whom he had met, one in particular:

> All the Padres I met were good men, but there was something different about Capt. Lynn. The most foul-mouthed chap in the companies was pleased to call him a friend. I think it was his kindly interest and thoughtfulness for every man in the Battalion, regardless of sect or creed, which made him such a favourite with us all. I know I felt he was a man doing a grand job in accordance with the views he must have felt when he was ordained.

Sapper Garfield Powell, brought up to attend church occasionally in his native Cardiff, received a kindly letter from his home church which 'after talking a lot of the usual rot' offered to confer on all their 'soldier adherents the boon of a fortnightly letter'. He was in a quandary: they would expect a reply in like terms, but like many of his fellow soldiers in France he had felt the strain of the contrast between the innocent values of home and those of the war zone:

> What am I to do? I am not sincerely religious and care not a rap for theology as they teach it. As far as I can see at present I am like all my friends — an agnostic. Most of my friends are Church members and are therefore hypocrites as well. Shall I tell them that I am trying to believe but cannot or shall I tell a lie? I'll temporise.

Many, particularly among front-line soldiers, finding what was happening around them disturbingly out of tune with the standard assumptions of Christianity, consciously or otherwise put conventional beliefs on hold 'for the duration', opting for a trench fatalism of which the essential credo was that if there was a bullet with your name on it you wouldn't survive, if there wasn't, you would. Yet it should be added that there were

97   *Questioning, or merely curious?   A British soldier contemplates a street-side crucifix at Fleurbaix, near Armentières. (Q690)*

countless others who came through the war with their faith unimpaired, men to whom such questions as 'Why doesn't God stop the war?' seemed irrelevant or even naïve. Yet some challenging of beliefs and a sense of profound spiritual shock were bound to occur in a conflict of such enormity, of which the essential act appeared to be the continuing sacrifice of the best youth of the combatant nations. Wilfred Owen's vision, in his poem 'The Parable of the Old Men and the Young', of an Abraham who spared the ram 'but slew his son/ And half the seed of Europe, one by one', was daring, shocking, but brilliantly apposite. George Morgan, 60 years after, put the same point in his own way: 'Such splendid youth: it seemed such a pity that they had to be killed.'

16 'Guerre finie! boche napoo!'

The war had been in progress for almost three years when Second Lieutenant E. J. Ruffell, 342 Siege Battery, Royal Garrison Artillery, saw the front line for the first time. It was in that depressing part of the fighting zone where the trenches ran through the coal-mining area centred on the industrial town of Lens. Ruffell was taken to an Observation Post in a ruined pit-head:

> Cautiously crawling up ladders which had more rungs shot away than remaining we at last came out on a small platform with sandbag sides and with a $\frac{1}{4}$-inch steel plate on the outer wall and we observed through holes made by shell splinters. I shall never forget the disappointment of my first view of the 'front' — shell pocked ground, ruined houses, rusty barbed wire everywhere and a maze of trenches and No Man's Land — not a soul to be seen, and not a sound except a solitary 'plop' of a sniper's rifle. And yet hundreds of men were living in those trenches and hundreds of eyes were watching for the slightest movement on either side — the slightest exposure over the top of a trench and 'plop' goes the sniper's rifle, and another man gets a 'blighty' or is sewn up in his blanket.

A greater source of disappointment for anyone who had held these trenches in the early days of the war would have been that after so many months the line was still where it was. To begin with it had been possible to hope that the Western Front was a temporary phenomenon only, that what Henry Williamson was to call 'that great livid wound across Europe' would soon be healed. Now such hopes seemed threadbare indeed. As early as August 1916 Driver R.L. Venables, echoing a widespread point of view, had written in his diary: 'When the war began everybody thought it would be over in a few months, now we are wondering if it will be ended in our lifetime.' Almost a year later relatively little had happened to counter such pessimism.

A major shift in the log-jam was, in fact, just about to happen. On 7 June 1917 — probably the very day that Ruffell climbed his rickety ladder and looked down on the front line — the British seized the Messines Ridge after the explosion of 19 mines: it was, for once, almost a walk-over. This was to be the overture to the Big Push of 1917.

Flanders was the place chosen for the great set-piece attack that year. The attacking battalions went over the top on 31 July. Like the Somme, this battle was to continue with small gains and huge losses until November. Like the Somme, it was to become the subject of fierce controversy at the time and unceasing argument ever after. Officially

98   *New weapon, impossible conditions: a tank stuck fast in the mud of Passchendaele.*
      (CO 2241)

known as the Third Battle of Ypres, it was to achieve its bitter fame under the name of the
little Belgian village which represented the farthest point of the British advance,
Passchendaele.

   This was to be a battle in which — even more than on the Somme — rain and mud
were to prove a crucial belligerent, and they were not on the British side. Hindenburg
even felt 'a certain feeling of satisfaction when this new battle began'. Experience had
shown that with the onset of the wet season 'great stretches of the Flanders flats would
become impassable, and even in firmer places the new shell holes would fill so quickly
with ground water that men seeking shelter in them would find themselves faced with the
alternative, "Shall we drown or get out of this hole?" This battle too must finally stick in
the mud.'

   The wet season began on the first day of the attack, causing an immediate setback after
early success. 'Had we only had a dry wicket we could have forced the Hun to follow on,
as it was the rain came down and the match had to be abandoned': thus the comment of
Lieutenant A.C. Wilkinson, 2nd Coldstream Guards. The abandonment was only
temporary; all autumn the British fought slowly forward, while, in Churchill's words, 'the
vast crater fields became a sea of choking fetid mud in which men, animals and tanks

floundered and perished hopelessly'. The tank, introduced first on the Somme the previous September, had struck terror in the Germans, whose reaction had been that 'The Devil is Coming', but its hour was yet to come; at Third Ypres it was as much a victim as all the other elements of war clogged in that rain-sodden countryside.

This battle produced much bitterness among the men who fought it. There was no place for idealism or even humanity in this brutal, bludgeoning campaign.

> There's no manœuvre, it's only batter the enemy — if you kill them we go forward a little, if not, we don't. Surely a private or a gunner could do that. It's not brains: it's blood. I never thought that we, British, would allow our good boys to be put in such a slaughter as this, so callous. No one thinks of another's life now, it's his own and to hell with everybody.
>
> *Gunner Hiram Sturdy, 162nd Brigade, Royal Field Artillery*

Private Jack Sweeney was almost distraught when he wrote to his fiancée in the last week of the battle:

> Our boys are having a terrible time in the trenches, up to the Waist in Mud and Water. Just like a ditch full of water. Each side of the Menin Road there are dead horses and men, cars, motor lorries in their hundreds, it is death to go off the road, as the mud is so deep. It is nearly death as it is as he is shelling all along the road . . .
>
> The Somme was bad enough but this is a thousand times worse.

This agonizing second half of 1917 was a hard season on the Western Front. It was at this time that Captain Dible, RAMC, expressed his profound concern over the matter of home leave. Leave, however, was only one part of what he saw as a general and growing disaffection — a malaise that had its own roots quite apart from the horrors of the battlefield. It is significant that he wrote the following at Étaples, where the notorious base camp and 'Bullring' had earned not a less but a more objectionable and tyrannical image as the war went on:

> Men, accustomed to what the Englishman has fought for for generations, personal freedom, are suddenly deprived of this greatest of possessions. They are being worked seven days a week for long periods without rest or change. The strain is wearing tempers thin, and the breaking point is often very near. Anomalies of pay are proverbial and staring. (Two men in the ASC working side by side on the same job may receive 6/— and 2/6 per diem respectively depending upon the different periods at which they enlisted; and the man who enlisted first is often the worse paid.) The tobacco ration is deficient. Officers and NCOs are often unable to differentiate between discipline and tyranny. These and a hundred other smaller matters are jarring on already rawed nerves.
>
> There the matter stands. What is being done? Nothing. There are two schools which have sprung into notice during the last week, in which some

definite trouble has shown itself here in Étaples. The one school says 'Bring down a couple of battalions and shoot the swine!' 'Send a regiment of cavalry to charge through them.' 'Stick them up against a wall, etc. etc.' That is the attitude of the old time soldiers. I am convinced that it is a fatal and suicidal one: you cannot treat the Englishman like that. Your battalion might refuse to shoot or your cavalry to charge. You cannot take the risk. The other school says: 'Find out what are their grievances and remedy them' and that is the only modus operandi to which I can subscribe. I confess I have every sympathy with the men.

The simmering discontent has recently come to a small head in this area. It began with the killing of an inoffensive man by an excited military policeman: developed into an outburst which swept every policeman out of the district and resulted in some of them being badly mauled in the process: and culminated in the temporary abolition of all discipline. Confusion reigns in all the camps and rank insubordination in some of them. It is a sign of the times. A small upheaval indicative of the potential volcano below the seemingly firm crust. The volcano is more than potential, it exists and is actively working: whilst the higher powers seem to live in total ignorance of, and are certainly outwardly ignoring, its existence.

1917 was the year of mutiny in the French Army. A policy by the future Marshal Pétain of simultaneously improving conditions and executing ringleaders without compunction restored the situation by the end of the year. The British Army avoided the ultimate crisis but certainly was not without its strains and crises.

Meanwhile the Third Battle of Ypres was closed down after the capture of Passchendaele by the Canadians on 6 November. This was followed shortly by the brief elation of Cambrai, on 20 November, when nearly 400 tanks, in the most dramatic strike of that new weapon in the war, broke through the German line and advanced five miles. The next day church bells rang out in London for the first time since the start of the war, but within days German counter-attacks put the line back much where it had been before.

On 31 December Captain Dible was once more confiding his distress to his commonplace book:

The war is getting more and more desperate. On every hand one sees unrest and dissatisfaction rampant and nothing sensible done to ameliorate grievances. We are living on a magazine.

A few weeks later Private Archie Surfleet was describing the same mood, though in terms perhaps more world-weary than alarmist:

February 8th. We have been in camp near the wood at Écurie for some days now and a more miserable existence it would be hard to imagine. There is nothing but unrest and uncertainty and everyone here is absolutely fed up to the teeth.

99   *Trench scene, January 1918: men of the 1/4th Battalion East Lancashire Regiment in a sap-*
head at Givenchy. By this time the world of the trenches had acquired an air of permanence.
'Open warfare' would begin its slow reappearance two months later, with the great German
attack of 21 March, but serving in 'the trenches' would always be the essential experience of
Western Front life. (Q6474)

But the perspectives of the war were changing. America had been a belligerent, if to begin with at a distance, since April 1917. The shift of her almost limitless potential from a benevolent neutrality to active participation on the Allied side meant that ultimate victory was all but guaranteed. In addition Germany was suffering crucially, both on the battlefield and, most painfully of all perhaps, by blockade. Her leaders were, however, by no means defeated. They resolved on a massive offensive on the Western Front to bid for victory before the Americans could affect the balance of power. The 'Kaiser's Battle', as the Germans called it, was launched on 21 March 1918 — and its principal target was the British Army. The attack began with a brief hurricane bombardment, with the initial strike upon the British batteries, strong points and command posts.

Second Lieutenant E.J. Ruffell's 342 Siege Battery took part of the brunt of the first onslaught:

> I was awakened at 4 a.m. by the most terrific gunfire I have ever heard. Only by shouting on the phone could I find out that all Batteries were answering on SOS Targets. The front line was one blaze of exploding shells and high

bursting shrapnel. 'Very' lights and every coloured rocket imaginable. Long range guns were 'sweeping' the back areas and about ten minutes after the firing started a shell burst just outside our dug-out and blew up all the telephone lines to Corps HQ and to Batteries!

As none of our Infantry were seen we concluded they had been wiped out . . .

This was a time when not a few battalions disappeared virtually without trace. Tom Macdonald's 9th Battalion of the Royal Sussex Regiment was more fortunate: it managed to squeeze clear of the German attack:

We were ready to defend our position, when further along to our right the Germans were pouring through and getting around behind. We had orders to pull out and as we retired to the road there were big cracks as ammunition shell dumps were exploded and it was an inferno.

We got back to dead ground. The remnants of us formed up and were marching when some Brass hat came from nowhere and our CO ordered about turn and we were put in a small wood to hold it. All were fed up and hungry, no rations. We were told it was a planned retreat and the cavalry were to close in on flanks. All propaganda to cheer us up. I think a lot were destroyed on the first day. Half the time one did not know where our front was, as the Germans were putting all the force in one sector and working around behind. You could see the Very lights going up in daylight behind us to signal to their artillery where they had got to.

Having avoided the German net Macdonald's battalion pulled back to a town which had just been hurriedly evacuated by its panic-stricken population:

They had left in a hurry. It was a sad sight really. Furniture etc. in houses was intact and clothing too. The men went wild with looting. They killed a calf and were cooking lumps of it and searching through the drawers for little pots of food, rice, etc. Hoarded down in the cellars under the houses were stacks of black bottles, I think it was cider. Of course they were all having their fill, lying on good beds with all filthy clothes and boots. They killed all the fowls catching them at night by light when they were on the perches.

The Germans advanced 30 miles in a week and almost reached Amiens. The 1916 Somme battlefield was totally engulfed. But the British, though they yielded, did not break and by the end of the month the worst threat was over. Fierce fighting, however, continued well into April with prodigious losses. In the month following 21 March 1918 the British sustained 250,000 casualties, as many as those at Passchendaele.

The same scenario would be repeated several times that spring: massive German attacks, a huge initial impact, a running out of steam as supply lines were stretched too far and the attacking troops lost energy and will. Now began the slow but final turning of the tide. The historic moment came on 8 August, when the British, using tanks as the spearhead with the infantry advancing behind, and with the support of a large number of aircraft, punched an 11-mile gap in the German line. Following this 'black day of the German Army' (Ludendorff's phrase) the enemy was forced steadily backwards; but the price was always high and the enemy's spirit by no means broken.

Captain Lionel Ferguson, 13th Battalion Cheshire Regiment, was a participant in this hard August fighting. On 21 August — it was a not unfamiliar situation — his battalion found itself advancing under 'hellish' machine-gun fire:

> We could find no cover or trench of any kind and we were walking through a hailstorm of MG bullets. Men fell right and left and we were quite unable to give them the attention required . . . I noticed one of the men threw down his rifle and equipment, which angered me greatly but before he had time to run I forced him to put them on again, in fact if he had hesitated I would have shot him and he knew it.

Yet earlier that day Ferguson had seen a portent of the future nature of land war. Advancing through the fog of that summer morning

> we overtook a large tank which had lost direction. The officer in charge was inclined to let the fog clear: but I informed him that a number of our troops were ahead and that we must press on. An enemy MG opened up on our right at that moment, and the old tank went right for it, firing a round of big shot as it advanced: we stopped to watch the scrap, a sight for all the world like a big dog going for a rat: the MG was firing the other way and before the Boche gunners had time to escape, the huge monster was upon them, finishing them for ever. It was the first blood we had seen that morning and for us spectators a most thrilling moment.

Then on Saturday 24 August he had a glimpse of the kind of war envisaged in pre-Somme days:

> The Cavalry were now going forward in large numbers, and we have lived to see the day of the cavalry in action. Every moment of the last few days has been wonderful and we feel we are making history.

Now at last the Allies were moving towards the end game. In September Walter Vignoles, formerly of the Grimsby Chums, now a Lieutenant-Colonel with his own Battalion, the 9th Northumberland Fusiliers, wrote to his wife:

> It is very interesting in the front line just now; continually chasing the Boche, moving forward every day, no billets, no shelters, everyone just sleeping under hedges or in shell holes. The Boche is burning all the farms, and as three-quarters of a French farm is wood it doesn't leave much. There is no doubt that Fritz is in a great mess.

100 *A Tommy of the King's Liverpool Regiment photographed next to a German signboard reading 'Kronprinzenstr.' — 'Crown Prince Street' — an indication that Britain and her Allies were finally achieving their goal and removing the Germans from the territories they had occupied for four years. Inchy, near Le Cateau, 13 September 1918. (Q7065)*

101 *18 September. A sergeant and two privates relaxing on ground near Epéhy, between Péronne and Cambrai, captured after hard fighting by the 12th Division earlier that day. (Q11326)*

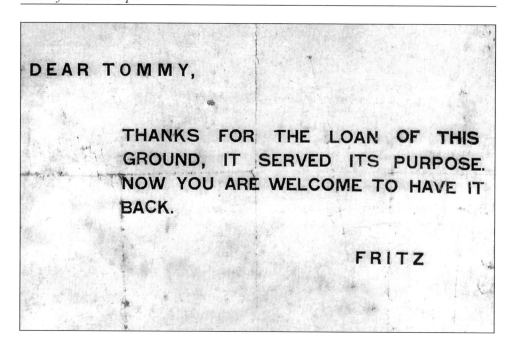

102 Fritz bids his old enemy farewell: a notice left in a German dugout near Bailleul, October 1918. (HU 59492)

At the end of September the Hindenburg line was broken. The advance continued against the background of the political disintegration of Germany and the first suggestion of an armistice.

> October 1918. Gerry was falling back and we were following on. The barrage was timed, so we were told, for 4 o'clock next morning. We stayed up waiting. It was a beautiful moonlit night. I had a watch with me and I remember a few of us were on the top of a hill to see what happened. At exactly 4 o'clock one gun fired — and then all the guns opened up all the way along the line, and there was a curtain of fire from horizon to horizon as far as the eye could see. It really was a magnificent sight. I remember someone saying, 'Not a cat could live in a barrage like that'. I suppose the fire-curtain wasn't above a man's height from the ground, but it was intense and continuous and accompanied by the non-stop roar of the guns. So there we stood with this world of moonlight around us and this world of flame in front, until the sun came up. That was a marvellous sight — the rising sun behind the curtain of flame; and as the sun gained in power the curtain of flame seemed to get ever paler, until in the full light of day it almost died out.
>   We moved on again after that.
>   *Private W. G. Brown, 2/3rd Field Ambulance, 59th (North Midland) Division*

On 23 October Lieutenant Ruffell's battery trundled into Solesmes:

> Up to this point in the advance, the Germans had driven the French civilians back with them, but this last push was rather too much for the Hun and he left the inhabitants in Solesmes and having evacuated the town, promptly shelled it. The poor French people were pathetically grateful to us and their tales of Hun brutality were horrible — for the first time we realized that the newspaper reports of brutality etc. were quite true and in fact — very mildly written.
>
> It was very embarrassing at first for us, for whenever a British officer passed a 'Civvy' — the 'Civvy' stepped into the gutter and removed his hat 'profoundly' (German order). We felt that this was not due to gratitude, and on questioning them, found that it was the result of four years of Hun discipline. Of course, we stopped this practice.

There was vigorous and sacrificial fighting right up to the end. It was on 4 November, just one week before the Armistice, that Lieutenant Wilfred Owen was killed at the crossing of the Sambre and Oise Canal, with the unhappy consequence that his parents received the telegram announcing his death as the bells of peace were ringing on 11 November. For Lieutenant Alex Wilkinson, 2nd Coldstream Guards, it was by contrast a good time. He wrote to his father on 6 November that the battle in which he had just been engaged was

> the best I have ever had and I would not have missed it for anything . . . We were right on top of the Huns before he could get his MGs to work and we got a nice few prisoners and MGs straight away. And a nice few Huns were killed there too. I had sworn to shoot the first one I saw, but I could not bring myself to do it. I am a sentimental ass. Having sent the prisoners back, on we went at a tremendous pace. The men were perfectly splendid, and showed amazing skill in the use of their Lewis Guns and rifles . . . But what I call the battle discipline left a great deal to be desired. The men got out of their formation unless carefully watched, and were inclined to lose direction, and too much time was wasted searching prisoners not only for arms but also for souvenirs. Even so it was most amusing to see practically every man smoking a cigar after we had passed the first objective . . .
>
> I think it is safe to say that it cannot be much longer. The Huns we met were certainly nothing to fear, and they thought of nothing but peace. They fully realized that they were absolutely beat to the world.

And then at last, from its ultimate source in the woods of Compiègne, where the German plenipotentiaries had been brought to sign the Allies' uncompromising armistice terms in a carriage of Marshal Foch's command train, the expected news came.

103 *The Canadians liberated Mons — scene of the first British fighting of August 1914 — on the day the war ended. Gunner J.H. Bird attached to Canadian forces wrote: 'During the afternoon a Band belonging to the Canadians played in the square and the inhabitants kept cheering and throwing wreaths of flowers at the bandsmen. You have no idea of the delight of these people.' (CO 3617)*

On the 11th November at about 8 a.m. we received a wire from Corps HQ to say that 'at 11 a.m. hostilities would cease, but no fraternization etc. would take place'. 11 o'clock came, and a sudden silence!
It was impossible at first to realize that the war was over. About 11.30 a.m. we realized that it was no longer necessary to wear our steel hats or gas masks!

So Lieutenant Ruffell ended his war.

Monday 11 November 1918 was one of the most remarkable days of modern times: 'the greatest day in the world's history', Queen Mary described it in her diary. Shortly before 11 o'clock the Prime Minister, Mr Lloyd George, emerged from 10 Downing Street and spoke to a boisterous, flag-waving crowd. 'It is over!' he said. 'They have signed! The war is won!'

On the stroke of 11, the capital went wild with joy. Maroons exploded, the 'All Clear' was sounded from the plinth of Nelson's column in Trafalgar Square and, in Churchill's words, 'the strict, war-stained, regulated streets of London became a triumphant pandemonium'. Crowds thronged the approaches to Buckingham Palace and when the King and Queen appeared on the palace balcony they were vociferously and repeatedly cheered. The weather deteriorated as the day wore on, but nothing could spoil the ardour of a people released from 52 months of war. That night the lights went on for the first time in many months. There were bonfires and fireworks. The theatres, restaurants, buses and

104 *Certificate of demobilization — for those who survived. [IWM Dept of Documents]*

The King commands me to assure you of the true sympathy of His Majesty and The Queen in your sorrow.

He whose loss you mourn died in the noblest of causes. His Country will be ever grateful to him for the sacrifice he has made for Freedom and Justice.

Milner

Secretary of State for War.

105 *Royal sympathy — for those who fell [IWM Dept of Documents]*

106 *Gravestone — for those whose bodies could not be identified. (Shirley Seaton)*

tubes were thronged with revellers. But here and there across the nation were those who did not celebrate, for whom the coming of peace brought home more bitterly than before the thought of loved ones and friends whom the war had taken away. One such was Robert Graves, poet and soldier, who went walking alone along the dyke above the marshes of Rhuddlan 'cursing and sobbing and thinking of the dead'. Another was Vera Brittain, who had lost a fiancée and a brother killed, and who walked through a carousing capital with her heart 'sinking in a sudden cold dismay'. For as she looked on the 'brightly-lit, alien world' around her, she realized the unhappy truth that 'as the years went by and youth departed and remembrance grew dim, a deeper and ever deeper darkness would cover the young men who had once been my contemporaries'.

In some sectors of the front there was fighting right up to 11 o'clock. At Lessines a squadron of the 7th Dragoons was sent forward to attack a bridge over the River Dendre at 10.50 a.m., so that in the very last minutes of the war men fell for King and Country. Elsewhere artillery fire went on sporadically for some time after 11 o'clock, as various batteries vied with each other for the distinction of firing the last shell. By midday or thereabouts, silence fell.

Men received the news of the cessation of hostilities in a variety of ways. For many there was unashamed relief; for others a numbed incredulity; yet others felt dismay that their victorious advance was to be halted just as they had got the enemy on the run. For Major R.S. Cockburn, now with the 63rd (Royal Naval) Division, who were, as he put it, 'probably nearer to Berlin than any other British troops', the news of the Armistice was 'as if the sun had forced its way through a bank of cloud'. But, he added, in his letter describing the occasion, 'on the whole the men took it philosophically. One of them said to me, "Well, that *is* a good thing, sir, isn't it!"'

As for the others whose experiences have been important in the making of this book, it is perhaps worth attempting to say where some of them were on this most memorable and longed-for of days.

Lionel Ferguson was in England nursing a Blighty wound received in the fighting of October 1918.

Tom Macdonald was learning to be an instructor at an Army Training School at Berkhamsted and having a hard time with his Sergeant-Majors.

Roland Mountfort, after serving for some months in British East Africa, was training in an Officer Cadet Battalion, and would receive his commission in March 1919.

Archie Surfleet was undergoing training as a pilot in the Royal Air Force.

George Morgan, now a Sergeant, was taking new recruits through a musketry course at Whitley Bay. The moment the news came through training was abandoned and everybody drank 'pints galore' in the canteen.

Thomas Bickerton, who had been captured in the March 1918 attack, together with a crowd of other prisoners of war, 'dirty, lousy and uncared for', was making his way on foot towards the Allied lines, having been sent packing by German guards only too glad to get rid of their wartime responsibilities. When he and his comrades finally reached friendly territory they formed fours and marched proudly down the road singing 'It's a long way to Tipperary' at the tops of their voices.

Jack Sweeney, walking down the main street of a village in Nottingham, saw the flag being raised over the local church and hearing that the bell-ringers were at work he and five others got together and rang the bells ('or at least made a terrible noise') for an hour and then went and had a drink.

Cyril Drummond was outside Buckingham Palace. He and everybody else in uniform had to stand at attention for what seemed like an hour while the Guards Band at the Green Park gateway played the national anthem of every possible ally. 'When at last the final one had been played and we all took our hands down the whole area around the Victoria Memorial suddenly became a sea of waving white handkerchiefs.'

Arthur Hubbard was serving as a Sergeant in the King's African Rifles in Nairobi. This for him was a happy time, but he would never recover from the effects of his war service and would take his own life a little over 10 years later.

Hiram Sturdy, home in his native Scotland and having survived a bout of influenza, went to Glasgow and saw 'singing, dancing, yelling people . . . the pent-up feelings of four years of waiting, sorrow, loneliness, misery, wickedness, crimes and cruelty of unbelievable magnitude being sung, drunk and danced out.'

Cyril Rawlins, who had suffered a severe head injury in a minor railway accident while working as his battalion's transport officer, was convalescing in England but would never be restored to full health.

Henry Bolton, George Buxton, Willie Clarke, Harry Farlam, Edgar Foreman, Kenneth Garry, Roland Ingle, Reginald Leetham, Kenneth Macardle, Peter McGregor, J.H. Mahon, Ian Melhuish, Wilfred Nevill and Robert Sutcliffe were dead. So too were more than a million other men from Britain and her Empire who had gone to war between 1914 and 1918.

107 Memorial to the Missing of the Somme, Thiepval, winter. (Author)

Envoi

When I go back there I feel I'm on consecrated ground. That ground has been trod by all those lovely lads who never came back.

I think that poem

> They shall grow not old, as we that are left grow old:
> Age shall not weary them, nor the years condemn.
> At the going down of the sun and in the morning
>> We will remember them.

I think it's marvellous. Because that's just how it is. You imagine them as they were then — not as they would be now — young, and in their prime, and never grown old.

George Morgan, former Bradford Pal, died 1977

Acknowledgements

In addition to certain key acknowledgements in the Preface, I should like to express my great gratitude for the help received from numerous individuals and institutions in the preparation of both the original and this revised new edition. BBC Television supported me in 1976 in the making of the TV documentary *The Battle of the Somme,* in researching for which much of the material included in the book came to light. J.M. Dent & Sons Ltd and its then directors, Peter Shellard and Malcolm Gerratt, enthusiastically commissioned the first edition. Crucial to both editions has been the co-operation of the Imperial War Museum's Department of Documents and Photograph Archive; one improvement in this one is that reference numbers have been assigned to all photographs from the latter source. The Art Department has given generous help in the selection of images for this edition's colour section. Numerous other illustrations came originally from private individuals, with many of whom I have sadly lost contact. My gratitude to them nevertheless; and also to Mme Gaby Antony for permission to use a photograph from the rich resources of Antony of Ypres.

Others I wish to thank include my wife Betty for undertaking a range of invaluable tasks including the checking of the typescript and proofs and assisting with the Index; Julie Robertshaw of the Museum's Department of Printed Books for reading the typescript; my son-in-law James Rowles for crucial help in mastering the mysteries of a new technology; and Kate Adams of Tempus for her expert work in setting the text and placing the illustrations.

My greatest gratitude, however, must be to my 'contributors'. In 1978 I wrote:

> The basic elements of this book were created 60 years ago on the Western Front, which is just another way of saying that the most important acknowledgment of all must be to the soldiers themselves, who, frequently in conditions of squalor and danger, wrote the remarkable letters and diaries on which *Tommy Goes To War* is largely based. With them I must include the ex-soldiers who in their memoirs and reminiscences tried to capture after the war the essence of their experiences during it. My gratitude to these men cannot be overstated. And from this it follows that my second most important acknowledgment must be to the people who preserved these letters and diaries and memoirs . . . realizing that they were not mere ephemera to be glanced at and thrown away, but that, quite apart from their personal value, they were the stuff of history.

That statement is equally valid today, with the rider that the figure '60' in the first sentence should now of course read 'over 80'. As to the copyright holders in the material used, every effort has been made to inform them of the new edition but the passage of time has made this no easy task. I offer my sincere gratitude to them all whether known or unknown, together with my hope that the goodwill shown to the first edition will also be granted to its successor.

Index

List of soldiers quoted